Living with Lyme Disease

Self-help for coping with the
challenges of chronic and post-Lyme

Helene Brecker

foreword by Donna Eden

ISBN-13: 978-1517353506

Dedication

This book is dedicated to my father, Sam Brecker, who lit the spark and empowered me by making me aware of the mind/body connection, and for his encouragement to take career risks. And to my husband, Bob Lavery, who supports who I am and all that I do. Thank you. I love you both.

Gratitudes

Go to Tsuneo Kaneko for piquing my interest in Shiatsu, Zen Buddhism, and Traditional Chinese Medicine; my doctor, Morgan Vittengl, MD; my Eden Energy Medicine teachers, Donna Eden and Vicki Matthews, ND, and colleagues Carrie Cummins, Carol Lovelee, Susan Shanley, Jack Treiber, Robert Weissberg, MD, and all those unmentioned who helped in my journey to recovery.

Thanks to Shannon Flattery for the suggestion to write this book.

Thanks to the models, Yvonne DeCore, Sandy Kahlon, Bill Sommers, and Bob Lavery.

Thanks to my editor, Rachel Spensieri.

Photos by Bob Lavery
Cover art by Kerry Endres
Portrait by Deborah Neary
Computer Tech assistance by Jaiden Wood and Mark Delfs
Formatting by Jesse Gordon

How to use this book

I am offering this self-help book as a reference manual of holistic techniques to address some of the common symptoms and challenges of Lyme disease. Part I of the book offers some theories of Chinese Medicine, explains the modalities being used, and provides definitions of terms. Part II lists the systems affected and various energetic techniques to work with those challenges. You can look up the mental or physical challenge you are facing and try some of the suggestions offered.

The wonderful part of using energy techniques is that you have the tools right at hand, literally. Because you are using your hands you don't have to be so precise, like with acupuncture needles. If you use several fingers to hold points you will surely be on it. The skills being offered are also empowering you to help in your own healing. This complement to traditional Western Medicine offers a chance to help oneself. It is in no way meant to take the place of consulting with your physician or psychotherapist when faced with the challenges of Lyme disease.

Contents of Book

Dedication..iii

Gratitudes..v

How to use this book..vii

Foreword by Donna Eden..xi

My Story..xv

Introduction..xxi

Part I..23

Chapter 1, Traditional Chinese Medicine..................23

Chapter 2, Modalities offered....................................27

Chapter 3, Definitions...31

Part II..35

Chapter 4, Adrenals...35

Chapter 5, Anger..39

Chapter 6, Anxiety and Panic...................................47

Chapter 7, Arthritis...55

Chapter 8, Backache/Sciatica.....................................63

Chapter 9, Dampness..67

Chapter 10, Depression/Grief....................................71

Chapter 11, Facial Paralysis (Bell's Palsy)................79

Chapter 12, Fatigue/Fibromyalgia.............................81

Chapter 13, Fear...91

Chapter 14, Headaches...95

Chapter 15, Immune System and Spleen...................101

Chapter 16, Infection...107

Chapter 17, Insomnia/Sleep Disturbances.................109

Chapter 18, Joint Inflammation................................115

Chapter 19, Kidneys..117

Chapter 20, Liver..119

Chapter 21, Memory/Cognitive Challenges..................123

Chapter 22, Metabolism......................................131

Chapter 23, Muscles...135

Chapter 24, Neurotic Behavior...............................137

Chapter 25, Numbness (Emotional)...........................139

Chapter 26, Pain...141

Chapter 27, PTSD/Trauma.....................................143

Chapter 28, Stomachaches, Indigestion......................149

Chapter 29, Thyroid..155

Chapter 30, Water Retention..................................159

Chapter 31, Worry...163

Appendix...167

Afterthoughts...167

References...170

About the author...175

Foreword
by Donna Eden

Who would have thought that the bite of a common deer tick, barely visible to the eye, could cause such havoc in the human body! Yet 300,000 people in the United States who are bitten every year can attest to the debilitating power of this tiny creature and the Borrelia bacteria it transmits. While the symptoms of many individuals who contract Lyme disease can be managed with medication, for at least 100,000 of the new victims every year, it is not likely to be an easy journey.

First of all, Lyme disease can mimic 200 other illnesses, so it is a moving target for diagnosis. Left untreated, or if treatment does not take, it may start with skin conditions that are unrelated to the site of the original bite along with migrating pain in the muscles, joints, and tendons. Sleep disturbances, memory loss, and mood changes are not uncommon. Neurological problems – from dizziness to facial palsy to meningitis – may appear. Abnormal heart rhythms may also occur as the disease impacts the heart's electrical conduction system.

Over time, Lyme disease may become a chronic condition as the infection spreads throughout the body. If oral antibiotics are not effective, long-term intravenous antibiotics may be the next course of action, but they may not be able to prevent the infection from settling into the body's various tissues and organs. The most frequently invaded areas include the muscles, joints, brain, and heart. Permanent impairment of sensory and motor function may be accompanied by severe nerve pain radiating out from the spine, joint swelling and erosion, or arthritic-like pains. Psychological symptoms may also appear, including cognitive impairment, anxiety, panic attacks, and delusional behavior.

Helene Brecker was one of the 100,000 people each year whose symptoms could not be controlled by medication. I have watched her healing unfold, and it has been a poignant victory of the human spirit using human ingenuity to tackle an enormous challenge. Her body was her laboratory, the canvas on which she painted a moving picture of her return to health. Like many who have overcome a terrible disease after conventional remedies have not worked, she is passionate – in the tradition of the "wounded healer" – to bring what she has learned to others. This book not only describes her journey back to health, it leaves markers on the path that others can follow.

While you can find some mention on the Internet of using pulsed electromagnetic fields and other forms of energy medicine in treating Lyme disease, this is the first guide that systematically offers step-by-step hands-on instructions for addressing the illness from every angle I can imagine. Its 31 chapters address the roles of the immune system, infection, inflammation, metabolism, pain, the adrenals, the thyroid, the stomach, the spleen, the liver, cognitive impairment, depression, fatigue, fear, and many other pertinent topics.

For each topic, we are shown how to use a range of energy healing methods to address its inherent challenges. Among the methods featured are Shiatsu, acupressure, do-in, energy psychology, Traditional Chinese Medicine, and Eden Energy Medicine (I am proud to have had Helene as a student and now see her as an expert in the field.....especially where Lyme and autoimmune diseases are concerned). Part of the book's beauty is not only its thoroughness in its range of topics but its simplicity in providing easy-to-apply techniques, whether working with the chakras, the meridians, or other energy systems.

Living with Lyme Disease is a wonderful reference manual with succinct, cogent explanations and practical advice and instruction. For those afflicted with Lyme disease that does not respond to conventional treatments, the methods this book presents cannot only save you from years of helpless suffering, it can empower you to know that you can, indeed, heal yourself.

– Donna Eden
Ashland, Oregon
October 2015

My Story

This book came about because of lessons learned during my journey with Lyme disease in 2005. It includes things I did for myself and additional techniques that I learned from working with others. It was inspired by an interview for a documentary film by Shannon Flattery entitled, "The Lyme Altar." Here is my story.

In the summer of 2005, I was diagnosed with Lyme disease. It never entered my consciousness that my love of gardening and the outdoors would bring me anything but joy. I don't recall being bitten, but in retrospect, I do remember asking my husband to scratch a nagging itch on my right shoulder blade.

My journey began on a beautiful Wednesday. I felt a little feverish, yet I didn't feel ill. I went out to dinner, and in spite of the delicious food, I couldn't bring myself to eat. When I got home, I went right to bed and woke feeling fine. So I disregarded what I felt the day before as an anomaly.

That weekend, I noticed a red blotch on my left upper thigh, just a red area – no pain, but lots of heat. I showed it to a couple of physicians attending an energy medicine class with me. They said to watch it but had no information on what it might be or indicate. Two days later, my back was in great pain. I wasn't sleeping and was barely able to walk. In the meanwhile, my husband noticed a spot on my back, on the right side at the base of my scapula. I dismissed it and never even mentioned it to the P.A., who I saw for the incredible back pain. He prescribed painkillers, which I wouldn't normally take, but nothing else helped to relieve the pain.

About a week later, I was still in agony; nothing was helping, not even the drugs. I wasn't sleeping or eating now. I couldn't find a comfortable way to rest, so I paced most of the night, going from room to room and from bed to couch to bed. I was miserable. By now, the spot on my shoulder had grown to encompass my entire back. I rejected the idea of a bulls-eye rash because it wasn't that– instead, it was a large, thin, red outline with a flesh-toned center. The rash on my thigh had grown too and turned to a wrinkled, yellow, chicken skin texture.

At my next doctor's visit, my husband showed him a series of photos he had taken of my back and thigh. My back was outlined with a rectangle from shoulder to shoulder and down to my hips. The doctor immediately grabbed his prescription pad and wrote two "scripts" – one for a blood test and one for an antibiotic. I still didn't want to believe it; I *couldn't* have Lyme disease! Of course, the blood work proved I did. After two doses of antibiotics, the pain was gone, as was the rash. Now the real challenges began.

During those several weeks, I had lost muscle strength in my legs and needed a walker to get around. Even with the walker, my legs couldn't support me, and I fell several times, breaking some toes. It was always hard to stand up, but sometimes I even forgot how to stand and would tearfully ask my husband to help me. Getting ready for the day took an hour or more, and I felt helpless most of the time.

The one thing I could do was meditate and "hold points." In Eden Energy Medicine (EM) and Touch for Health, acupressure points are often used to sedate pain, so I was holding points a lot. I was also doing exercises and holding points to strengthen my Spleen and sedate Triple Warmer meridians since both help with building the immune system. I still wasn't sleeping much and had to go up our spiral staircase backwards in a seated position. I did this only once a day; it was too exhausting to do more often.

The turning point came when the in-home physical therapist evaluated my muscle strength. She said my quads and my psoas muscle (which connects the spine to the hip) were extremely weak. After she left, I began to hold acupressure points to strengthen the meridians that were associated with those muscles. Three days later at her next visit, I was able to lift my right foot off the ground and showed increased strength in those muscles. She was surprised at my progress. I continued to hold points as well as do the exercises she suggested. At the next visit, three days later, I was able to lift my leg well enough to drive my manual transmission car around our driveway. The walker was sometimes left behind. The PT was amazed at how quickly my muscles came back and closed my case. I was determined to be back to my old self quickly. Within a month of getting diagnosed, I was back to gardening on a chair, driving, walking, and cooking from a stool. Not quite my old self–but nearly.

I credit my rapid recovery to early detection, the proper medication, and Energy Medicine. Thankfully, my studies in Eden Energy Medicine introduced me to a wonderful group of people who came to my home – some did Reiki and some performed Energy Medicine techniques on me. Each time, I improved markedly. The first practitioner calmed my panicked mind using neurovascular points; now some of the fear that I would never walk again was gone. Another cleared and balanced my chakras. About a week later, another colleague came and did some energy balancing, and for the first time, I was able to walk down the stairs one foot after the other. I did my part by continuing to sedate meridians for pain, strengthen meridians and their associated muscles so I could get walking, and use neurovascular points to calm my very nervous mind.

I'm back in the garden and continue to hike. Now I'm more vigilant about dressing properly, checking for ticks, and I won't ignore a sudden fever or rash if I do get bit. Most importantly, I will continue to do my EM exercises to keep my energy systems balanced, keep my immune system strong, and calm my mind.

Introduction

One of the exercises I do daily and believe is essential to wellness is referred to in Eden Energy Medicine as the "Four Thumps." It involves tapping or rubbing the following points: the center of the cheek, **ST 1 "Tear Container"**; below the collarbone, **K 27 "Elegant Mansion"**; the center of the breastbone (thymus); and the last point on the Spleen meridian called "Great Embracement."

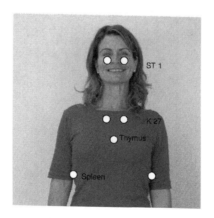

Another part of my daily routine is to make sure my energy is crossing over in my brain. I trace Xs across my body by firmly dragging my right hand over my left shoulder to my right hip and then alternating from right shoulder to left hip. I do it about 10 times on each side.

Another essential is hooking up my energies. This is done by putting one finger in your navel and the other at the third eye (the space between your eyes) and pulling up at both spots while taking several breaths. This connects two meridians, one that runs up the front of the body called Conception Vessel and the other which runs up the back called Governing Vessel. Often I will sigh or yawn when those meridians are connected. I usually do this before I get out of bed in the morning.

Part I

Chapter 1
Traditional Chinese Medicine

What is Traditional Chinese Medicine (TCM)? TCM is a many thousand years-old system of healing that is concerned with balancing Qi (pronounced *chee*) in the body. TCM incorporates many modalities like diet, lifestyle adjustment, exercise like Tai Chi or Qi Gong, meditation, acupressure or Shiatsu, massage, acupuncture, herbs, and moxibustion (the use of heat with a cigar shaped tube of mugwort or wormwood over an acupuncture point). TCM theory is based in nature. It looks at how the individual interacts with life and the environment, and is related to the seasons, weather, time of day, diet, and emotions.

TCM works with both the energy and physical structure of the body. Energy runs through energy pathways called meridians. There are special points along these meridians that have importance to balancing the flow of Qi. Balance is achieved when energy is unobstructed and can flow smoothly. There are 12 bilateral meridians running vertically in the body. They are named after the organs that their energy is connected to internally. There are also two other meridians: one runs up the front of the body from the perineum to the lower lip. The other runs up the back from the perineum up over the head and ends at the back of the throat.

TCM is also based on the yin-yang principle that nature is ephemeral and that two forces are always opposite and antagonistic and, at the same time, complementary, both combining and cooperating. Yin is contracting and dissipating. It is also passive. Yang force tends to be expansive and active. Maintaining equilibrium with these forces is necessary and is the key to wellness. Self-care is the number one method of maintaining this yin-yang balance.

"The key to mastering health is to regulate the Yin and Yang of the body." - Yellow Emperor's Classic of Medicine

TCM is also based on the Five Element theory, which reflects the rhythm of nature and relates to the seasons. Each season has a related element, taste, color, emotion, time of day, direction, climate, smell, sound, and yin/yang organs. They are:

	Winter	Spring	Summer	Late Summer	Fall
Element	Water	Wood	Fire	Earth	Metal
Color	blue/black	green	red	yellow	white
Emotion	fear/ anxiety	anger/ resenting	joy/sorrow	sympathy/ empathy	grief/worry
Time	3-7PM	11PM-3AM	11AM-3PM	7-11AM	3-7AM
Direction	North	East	South	Center	West
Climate	cold	wind	heat	moist	dry
Smell	putrid	rancid	scorching	fragrant	rotten
Taste	salty	sweet	bitter	sweet	pungent
Sound	groaning	shouting	laughing	singing	crying
Organ Yin/Yang	Kidney/ Bladder	Liver/Gall Bladder	Heart/ Small Intestine	Spleen/ Stomach	Lung/ Large Intestine

A bit about points

In TCM, and in Japanese medicine, characters making up a name for the point accompany the numbering system of points along a meridian. These names can suggest a spiritual or emotional application and are often considered vital to understanding the function of the point. Other points don't have that basis.

Some points have many names; others only one. Originally, only names were used, but because of differences in spelling and pronunciation, a wide variety of names evolved. Numbers came into use because people couldn't read the Chinese (Han) characters. In the 1990s, the World Health Organization standardized the numbers, so I've included the numbers I've learned, as well as the standardized ones in use now in parentheses. I've chosen to include the English translation of the point name because some are so descriptive and informative. For example, the translation for a Large Intestine point (LI 20) used to relieve nasal congestion, located at the flare of the nose, is "Welcoming Smell" or "Welcoming Perfume," an apt description of its function.

Chapter 2
Modalities offered

Shiatsu is Japanese for "finger pressure." **Acupressure** is the application of pressure (with the thumbs or fingertips) to the same points on the body used in acupuncture. To measure and locate acupoints on anyone's body, it's important to remember that everyone's body is of a different size and shape, so a person's personal measurements are used to locate points. When I was a student of Shiatsu, my teachers referred to a measurement of a cun, or body inch. There are two ways to do this. One is to measure the width of the person's thumb above the joint below the nail. The other is to measure the distance between the first and second joints of the person's third (middle) finger. The distances are about the same. I'm borrowing from www.tcmstudent.com for a measurement chart.

Pressure - When applying pressure to the body, often the pressure is firm. When holding strengthening or sedating points, or points on the head, the pressure is light, about the weight of a nickel. If you use several fingers on the area when holding a point you will certainly make contact with the one you want to hold.

Energy medicine takes practices from acupuncture, Touch for Health, yoga, and Qi Gong. It serves as a complement to other medical approaches and is a system of self-care and self-help. It includes working with the meridians and other subtle energy systems of the body.

Do-In means to "pull or stretch" and is an ancient form of exercise to improve physical, emotional, and spiritual health. It involves breathing, self-massage, and gentle pressure on the meridians to harmonize the body and the internal organs.

Energy psychology is a process of stimulating meridian points for emotional relief. These points, found on both sides of the body, are connected to the amygdala, the part of the brain related to our emotions. It involves light tapping on points to interrupt the electrical energy to and from the amygdala. A gentle rubbing or simple touch on the point is used also.

Another technique involves holding a point and breathing. Some techniques use set-up statements and affirmations, others just have the individual focus on the problem while tapping on various points, which are shown below. There are many tapping webinars and books available for your further study. Please see a qualified clinician for help with serious problems. You can experiment by tapping on the points shown below in succession or on a specific area for some relief from anxiety, pain, or trauma. Remember to breathe while you are tapping. Though points occur on both sides, you need only tap or hold each area on one side for it to be effective. Tap about six times, or hold for several breaths.

	Location	Meridian	Emotion
1.	Side of the hand	Small Intestine	Procrastination
2.	Beginning of eyebrow	Bladder	Sadness
3.	Side of the eye	Gall Bladder	Rage
4.	Under the eye	Stomach	Anxiety
5.	Under the nose	Governing	Embarrassment
6.	Under the lip	Central	Shame
7.	Collarbone	Kidney	Reversals
8.	Under the arm	Spleen	Fear of the future
9.	Ribcage	Liver	Old anger
10.	Thumbnail	Lung	Grief
11.	Index finger	Large Intestine	Guilt
12.	Middle finger	Pericardium	Allergens
13.	Little finger	Heart	Anger
14.	Valley/gamut point top of the head	Triple Warmer	Stress

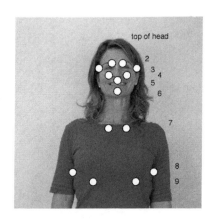

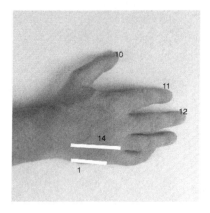

Chapter 3
Definitions

Chakras are from the yogic tradition and are considered energy stations. One article states chakras are parts of the body where the centripetal force of heaven and the centrifugal force of earth's core collide. There are seven major chakras (root, womb, solar plexus, heart, throat, third eye, and crown). Chakras carry your memories and different aspects of your personality, and are associated with the organs found near them.

The root chakra deals with survival and vitality and holds ancestral memories. It's connected to our lower digestive system.

Sacral or womb chakra is about creativity, pleasure, and projects. It's related to the adrenals, genitals, and urinary tract.

The solar plexus chakra deals with self-esteem, confidence, and willpower, and is where parental messages are imprinted. It is associated with digestion, the spleen, pancreas, kidney, and abdominal organs.

Heart chakra is about love, compassion, emotions, and peace. It's associated with our heart, thymus, breasts, shoulders, and blood circulation.

Throat chakra is about speaking your truth and communication and is associated with thyroid, parathyroid, cervical spine, and trachea. The throat chakra is special in that it holds information on all the other chakras and has seven chambers, which are each connected to a different chakras.

The third eye chakra deals with intuition, insight, and awareness. It's associated with the brain, pituitary, eyes, ears, and nose.

Crown chakra deals with divine energy, pure consciousness, and silence. The crown chakra is associated with the pineal gland, cerebral cortex, and hormones.

Meridians compose a set of pathways in the body where vital energy flows. These pathways are sometimes referred to as a river. There are 12 meridians, which occur on both sides of the body and begin or end in the fingers or toes. They are Lung, Large Intestine, Stomach, Spleen, Heart, Small Intestine, Bladder, Kidney, Pericardium, Triple Warmer, Gall Bladder, and Liver. There are two additional meridians, one that goes up the front of the body called Conception Vessel, and another going up the spine known as Governing Vessel.

Neurolymphatic points are reflex points, which correspond with their respective organs and that trigger the lymph system to release its waste for elimination. They are located predominantly on the body. Pressure used with these points is usually firm.

Our lymph system flows in one direction and serves as a drainage system for the body. It carries proteins, fats, and hormones to all the cells in the body. We have twice as many lymph vessels as blood vessels,but unlike the circulatory system, the lymph system has no pump. It needs exercise–movement like walking or massage–to create flow.

We can help the lymph flow by working the neurolympathic reflex points in the body. These points act like circuit breakers, and when the system is overloaded, they are usually tender. The tenderness is an indication of an imbalance in a meridian and associated muscles. Tenderness decreases as the balance returns to the muscle and the meridian.

These points are usually massaged deeply for 20 seconds. Start slowly though; you don't want to overwhelm your system with lymph—it could cause nausea or dizziness.

Neurovascular points are reflex points that connect the nervous system and circulatory system with the meridians. These points, usually occurring bilaterally, are located primarily on the head and are held lightly for 20 or 30 seconds. I use these most often when my problem stems from an emotional issue.

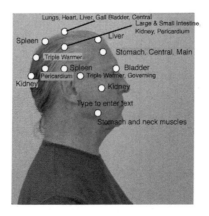

Part II

Chapter 4
Adrenals

The adrenals, which sit on top of the kidneys, produce or contribute to the production of vital hormones that affect every major bodily process. They are involved in our immune function and the body's response to stress. The adrenals regulate blood sugar, blood pressure, and inflammation. They mobilize the use of protein in the body and carry thyroid hormone from the blood to the cells. Lyme disease and other tick-borne infections can cause adrenal insufficiency. Infections weaken the adrenals making the individual more susceptible to health challenges.

Adrenals are governed by Triple Warmer meridian, which in Energy Medicine is our fight-flight (or freeze) response, and supports recovery from injury, illness, or general stress. Triple Warmer is a Fire element meridian.

Ways to strengthen the adrenals

Here is a very simple way to improve the function of the adrenals and Kidney meridian: allow the left hand to float up the back of the body with the center of the hand resting on the lower back behind the navel. This connects the Ming Men point (Gate of Life) behind the navel with the Lao Gong point (Palace of Labor) in the center of the palm.

The adrenals, along with the Kidney and the Heart meridians, are most affected by fear. This can affect brain function, especially memory. Avoiding or resolving stressful issues can restore balance to the adrenals and Kidney. A way to relieve fear is to place one hand on the forehead and the other hand at the base of the back of the head – called the frontal-occipital hold. While in this position, bring the fearful thoughts to mind and hold until you feel a pulsing in the fingers on your forehead and/or it becomes difficult to hold the fearful thought in your mind.

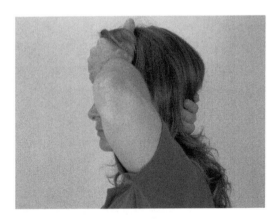

Another technique to strengthen the adrenals is to deeply massage the adrenal points, located one inch out and one inch above the navel for twelve to fifteen seconds.

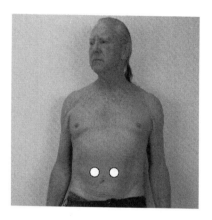

Triple Warmer governs the adrenals, so attending to the needs of Triple Warmer is a smart thing to do to help oneself. One of the ways to calm Triple Warmer is to place the thumbs at the temples and the fingers on the forehead. Lightly hold your fingers while you breathe slowly and deeply until you feel pulsing in the fingertips or you release a deep sigh, probably two minutes or so.

Another is tracing Triple Warmer meridian backwards. Start at your temple, going around the back of your ear, down your outer arm to your fourth finger.

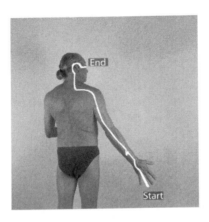

Chapter 5
Anger

Facing the challenges of a chronic illness brings up lots of feelings. Anger is definitely one of them, and that can be expressed in many ways such as anger towards: the tick, the quality of testing/care, the level of difficulty with daily life, etc. Anger is the emotion of Wood element, and it's associated with Liver (anger focused inward) and Gall Bladder (anger towards the outer world) meridians.

Sugar, fried foods, alcohol, or excess emotions are taxing to the liver; these are good things to avoid. Say yes to the chlorophyll found in green vegetables and to sour foods like lemon and sauerkraut when dealing with anger. Drink water when you feel angry; it will help cool you down. And literally take some time to "smell the roses." A scent that is relaxing helps to balance anger.

Anger causes the adrenals to produce stress hormones due to signals received from the brain. These can tax the digestive and cardiovascular systems. The constant bombardment of adrenal hormones weakens the immune system, especially if anger is not expressed in a healthy way. Too much anger—especially when it is repressed—can create chronic tension, irritability, migraines, hot flashes, and insomnia.

Creating space in the body helps to release energy and feelings, so stretch several times a day. Exercising or working hard is great for letting go of things that may be better left unsaid. One of my favorites for times like that is an exercise my friend calls "Fists of Anger." I always follow this with Zipping Up.

Fists of Anger

1. Stand with your fists at your sides and bring an angry thought to mind.

2. Swing your arms out to your sides and over your head as you inhale.

3. Quickly and with force, bring your fists down and blow out, sending the energy to the ground as you release your fists.

4. Repeat several times, quickly.

5. The last time, bring your hands down slowly and deliberately, and blow out slowly with force.

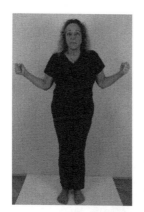

Zip Up

1. Place your hand at the bottom end of the Central meridian, at your pubic bone.

2. Take a deep breath in as you move your hand straight up the center of your body to your lower lip.

3. Repeat three times.

Acupressure points for anger

*   **GB 20 "Gates of Consciousness"** is at the base of the skull in the hollow between the large muscles in the neck. It helps with anger, frustration, stress, and tension in the neck and shoulders.

- **B 10 "Heavenly Pillar"** sits below the base of the skull about one-half inch on either side from the center hollow and can help to release repressed anger and stress.

- **GB 21 "Shoulder Well."** t the top of the shoulder two finger-widths from the side of the neck, helps with irritability, relieves excessive anger, and traditionally is used for arm and shoulder tension. *Avoid using this point if you are pregnant.*

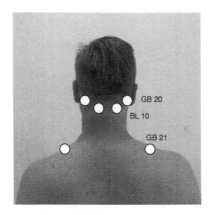

CV 12 "Central Venter" sits midway between the bottom of the sternum and the belly button. Holding this point relieves emotional stress and frustration. Best to hold this no longer than two minutes and to do it on an empty stomach. Be cautious and press lightly with this point if you have a serious illness like heart disease, cancer, or high blood pressure.

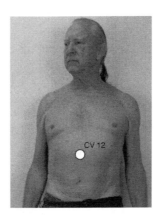

- **P 6 "Inner Pass,"** in the middle of the inside of the forearm three finger-widths from the wrist fold, is useful when feeling excessive anger.

- **P 9 "Central Hub"** is found on the inside base of the nail of the middle finger. Hold this point by squeezing your nail. It is an emergency revival point.

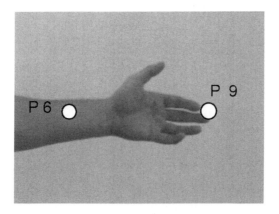

Another great way to deal with anger is to hold areas on your head related to Wood element, for example, holding your forehead and thinking about your anger. The idea is to shift your brain from anger into more rational and calmer thinking. Place your thumbs lightly on your temples with your fingertips on your forehead. Bring one thought that is creating anger into your mind. Continue to hold that thought as you hold your head. Hold until you feel pulsing under your fingertips. Blood will be coming into your forebrain, and you will begin to feel calmer.

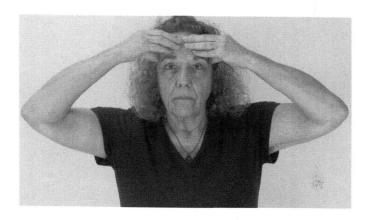

Chapter 6
Anxiety and Panic

My memory of the early days of my Lyme adventure is one of panic that I would never walk again. Then there were the feelings of heightened anxiety before simple activities, like worrying if I would be able to stay upright with the walker this time. (That came after falling to the ground when my legs and arms couldn't support me with the walker.)

Feelings of panic and anxiety can create breathing challenges. The posture of an anxious person changes—the chest caves in and compresses the area around the diaphragm. This causes shallow breathing. Reduced oxygen to the brain can leave you not thinking clearly and can weaken the lungs. When lungs are weakened, there is diminished health and vitality.

Reaction to real or imagined events or danger can cause us to go into fight-or- flight mode and bring with it muscle tension, headaches, fatigue, memory challenges, sleep disturbances, and poor concentration. Panic attacks, with that sudden overwhelming onrush of fear, increase the heart rate, make breathing difficult, and can leave a person shaking and sweating.

In TCM, anxiety is referred to as a Fire deficiency. The element associated with Panic is Fire. Balancing Fire element is important in calming those emotions. A way to do that is to gently hold points on the head that will help balance Fire and calm the sense of panic.

Place one hand on your forehead and the other hand at the bulge at the back of the head. While holding your head, allow yourself to sink into the feeling of panic. After a few minutes, you might become aware of pulsing in the fingers on your forehead or have trouble holding onto the feeling of panic or even begin to feel calm.

Another meridian in Fire element that goes into overdrive during those moments of fight, flight, or freeze is Triple Warmer. There are several easy ways to bring a sense of peace and calm to that meridian and your mind.

Triple Warmer Smoothie

1. Place your fingers at your temples. Take a deep breath.

2. On another deep in-breath, slowly slide your fingers up and around your ears.

3. As you exhale, slide our fingers down and behind your ears; press them down the sides of your neck, and hang them on your shoulders.

4. Push your fingers into your shoulders and drag them to the middle of your chest, with one arm resting on top of the other.

5. Hold there for several deep breaths.

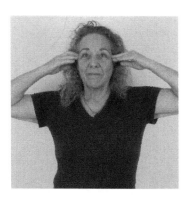

One of my favorites is a hug that calms your Triple Warmer while strengthening either your Spleen (left side) or Liver (right side).

Nurturing Hug

1. Wrap your left hand around your right arm, just above the elbow.

2. Wrap your right arm around the left side of your body, underneath your breast.

3. Hold this position for at least three deep breaths.

4. Switch the way your arms are wrapped around your body.

Another great way to calm an overactive Triple Warmer is:

1. Place your thumbs over your index fingers making on "O."

2. Place your thumbs at your temples. Gently place the middle finger and ring finger of each hand on the center of the forehead above the brows.

3. Hold this position, breathing deeply for one to two minutes. You may feel a pulse in your fingers. Hold the position until you feel calmer.

Helpful acupressure points

Lu 1 "Central Residence" – Place all your fingers on each side of your upper chest, your thumbs in the soft area near your shoulder. Hold firmly for about two minutes and breathe. This is a wonderful tool during a panic attack since it will comfort and soothe you and bring a sense of calm, quickly ending the sense of panic.

CV 17 "Sea of Tranquility" – Place your middle finger lightly on the center of breastbone. Hold it there while taking slow, deep breaths for a couple of minutes. It will open the chest for easier breathing and stimulate the thymus, relieving anxiety, nervousness, panic, and depression.

GV 24.5 "Impressive Palace" – Place your palms together, and let your middle fingers rest at your third eye while breathing slowing and deeply for two minutes, concentrating on your third eye. This stimulates hormones and neurochemicals through the pituitary to relieve anxiety and nervousness. It is also good for improving one's intuition.

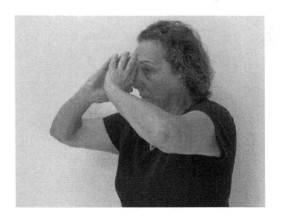

P 6 "The Inner Barrier" can help with anxiety and a racing heartbeat. It's found on the inside of the forearm, in the center about three finger-widths above the wrist crease.

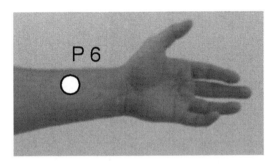

There are many modalities of energy psychology available to help with so many issues, anxiety being one of them. **See pages 29 & 30 for tapping points.** Focus on what you are anxious about as you tap these points. If your anxiety is severe, please seek out a therapist trained in Energy Psychology techniques.

Chapter 7
Arthritis

Many people, especially in the morning, face stiff joints along with joint swelling and pain from Lyme. In TCM, there are many contributors to this disease. All varieties are connected to a restriction or obstruction in energy flow, and pain is affiliated with obstruction. Tension and stress can lead to shortened muscles, inflammation, and restricted range of motion. If the joints are tense, movement becomes difficult.

One of my favorite ways to relieve obstruction is by moving and stretching. This exercise is wonderful for creating space and releasing excess energy, bringing fresh blood and oxygen to the cells and stimulating fresh energy into the joints. Donna Eden calls this "**Connecting Heaven and Earth**":

1. Rub your hands together briskly, and place your hands on your thighs, fingers spread. Feel the energy moving towards your feet, grounding you.

2. Deeply inhale through the nose. Circle your arms out and have your hands meet mid-chest in prayer position; exhale through the mouth.

3. Inhale; stretch one hand straight up, the other straight down. Flatten hands, fingers pointing away from the body, one pushing up to sky, the other pushing down to earth. Hold.

4. Exhale; return hands to prayer position. Repeat, switching arms.

5. Release pose, and fold body over at the waist. Hang there, knees slightly bent, for two breaths.

6. Return to standing slowly; as you do, make figure 8s with your hands up your body to your head. Let the energy roll down your back.

The Chinese system states that arthritis comes from an assault by four of the "Five Devils" or pathogenic influences – Wind, Damp, Cold, and Heat – on the body. Each type of influence has different symptoms.

Wind Devil affects Wood element and is associated with Liver energy. It is manifested with moving or migrating sensations of pain.

The following points can help alleviate pain associated with Wind:

- **Liv 3 "Great Rushing"** is found on the top of the foot in between the bones between the first and second toe. This will keep energy and blood moving and help to eliminate Wind.

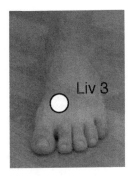

- **GV 12 "Pillar of the Body,"** located on the spine about shoulder level, eliminates Wind and strengthens the body, mind, and spirit. It supports the immune system and is good for the upper back, neck, head, and shoulder and elbow pain.

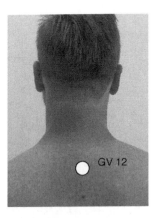

- **GB 34 "Yang Mound Spring"** can be found by running your finger up the outside of your leg until you hit a bony prominence under your knee. Gall Bladder 34 is located just slightly in front of and below where the bone juts out. It's very influential with tendons and sinew and is good for any condition involving injured or strained tendons. It supports joints and helps to ensure energy flow to muscles.

Damp Syndrome

Damp weather and barometric changes affect Earth elements and imbalances in Stomach/Spleen energy. Pain is made more intense at those times and is dull and heavy and localized. The following acupressure points can improve damp weather-related pain:

- **ST 36 "Three Mile Point"** is located about four finger-widths below the knee on the outside of the shin. Hold for about one minute. It strengthens the body, supports Stomach and Spleen function, helps with fatigue, and increases the metabolism to help burn off the dampness.

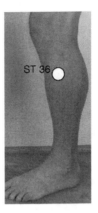

- **Sp 9 "Fountain of Yin Spring"** is located in the depression on the inside of the leg, just under the knee. This is usually very sensitive.

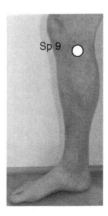

Cold Syndrome is associated with Kidney and Water energy. Pain is often felt as severe cramping with an intense penetrating feeling in one area. It is usually treated with heat—either wet heating pads or moxibustion—when an herb (usually mugwort) is burned over the affected area. This is not done when there is any inflammation.

A ginger compress is good for pain, bringing heat to and promoting circulation over the area. It's easy to make a ginger compress. Grate about five ounces of ginger root and place in a cheesecloth bag. Put into two quarts of warm water and heat until the water becomes a pale yellow. Soak a cloth in the warm water and place over the painful area. Again, do not do this when there is inflammation.

Heat Syndrome is considered a disturbance in yang energy. Large Intestine and Metal element are associated with this condition. Pain is often experienced as intense burning, with redness and swelling around the joint. A few points that can be helpful for this condition include:

- **GV 14 "Great Hammer"** is used to remove heat from the blood and is located on the base of the neck right below the seventh cervical vertebra.

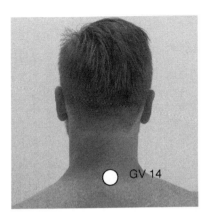

- **LI 4 "Great Eliminator"** is useful to disperse energy in the upper part of the body, especially the neck and head. It is located in the webbing between the thumb and index finger.

- **LI 11 "Crooked Pond"** also disperses heat and removes obstructions and helps with elbow pain. It's at the outside of the elbow crease when the arm is bent.

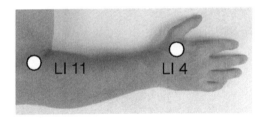

Chapter 8
Backache/Sciatica

One of the many drawbacks of being unable to get around can be the weakening of abdominal muscles. This makes the individual more susceptible to back, muscle, and ligament strains. Stress, accidents, and poor posture can also lead to backaches. The best way to cope with back pain is to move. Staying flexible is important, as well as keeping the abdominal and back muscles strong.

Clients often will call with questions about soothing a backache; usually I can offer an area to work on based on where they are feeling the most pain. My general rule for lower back pain is to rub the area between your waist and sacrum with the back of your fists. Also rubbing deeply along the outsides of the thighs from hip to knee can also ease back pain. Another area to focus on, especially for sore buttocks muscles, is the top of the pubic bone, as is rubbing the upper area of the inner thighs.

There's a wonderful point I learned about eons ago when I first learned Shiatsu; it was my go-to point when I was troubled with sciatica. It is called **Bl 60 "Name of the Mountains"** and is located in a depression midway between the outer part of the anklebone and the Achilles tendon. Holding this point, with strong pressure, for 10 seconds, three times on each foot, works wonders for temporarily relieving sciatica pain.

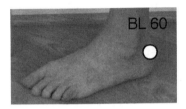

Bringing your knees to your chest is a good way to gently stretch the lower back and prepare it for deeper work. Take a breath in and exhale as you draw your knees up. Repeat several times, releasing your knees with each inhale.

More acupressure points to use are:

- **CV 6 "Sea of Energy"** is located about two finger-widths below the navel and helps with low back weakness as well as tones the abdominal muscles. Press into that spot about one to two inches, and breathe for one minute.

- **Bl 23** "Healing Point for the Kidney" and **Bl 47** "Sea of Vitality" (also called **UB 42** "Will Chamber") are on either side of your spine, across your lower back, around waist-level. They will be sensitive if you have lower back weakness. In that case, hold lightly for a few minutes. If it's not too tender, rub vigorously with your knuckles over the area. Then use your fingers to deeply massage the tight muscles on either side of your spine.

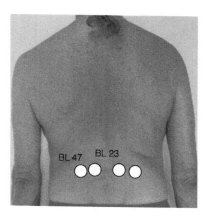

- **Bl 54** "**Commanding Middle**" (also known as **UB 40** "**Bend Middle**") can be found by placing your thumbs at the back of your knees. Rocking the legs back and forth for about a minute will relieve back pain and stiffness, and arthritis in the knees, back, and hips. Go gentle on this point, especially when helping another person.

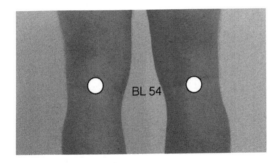

Chapter 9
Dampness

We are all familiar with the uncomfortable feeling of dampness, especially in late-summer when the air is heavy and moist. The humidity leaves you sticky, sometimes with swollen joints and limbs puffy with water retention. In proper amounts, dampness is nourishing, like when moist soil helps the seedlings grow or when the water found in fruits and vegetables provides us with sustenance. Our tissues, muscles, and skin need dampness to be supple. But too much dampness can cause rot and creates an optimal environment for yeast, mold, and fungi to grow. Examples of excess dampness are overripe fruit, rotting garbage, and foul breath.

In Traditional Chinese Medicine, Dampness is also an internal condition caused by excess worry. It inhibits the digestion, leading to a backup of undigested fluids. It is characterized by gas, sluggish stool, lack of appetite, lethargy, indecision about what to eat, inability to enjoy food, foggy thinking, concentration challenges, phlegm, and memory problems.

The condition of Dampness is worsened by dairy, starchy foods, fried or greasy foods, thyroid medication, and birth control. It can be dispelled with ginger, cayenne, and spicy foods. Things that create heat and dryness are helpful. Gentle, non-strenuous exercises like yoga, Tai Chi, swimming, and walking can be beneficial.

Since Dampness affects Earth element, doing exercises that balance Stomach and Spleen are helpful. This Do-In exercise balances both Earth element meridians — Spleen and Stomach.

Do-In

1. Sit on the ground on your knees with arms clasped overhead. Lower your body backwards towards the floor (eventually having the shoulders touching the floor) and take two deep breaths.

2. Change the position of your hands by having a different thumb on top. Take two deep breaths. Notice if there is a the difference between sides.

Strengthening Spleen meridian is an important activity to reduce Dampness. Spleen meridian starts at the outer corner of the big toe and travels up the inside of the leg, flares out at the hip, continues up to the armpit, and down to the bottom of the ribcage. For a quick burst of energy, you can tap on the Spleen points at the bottom of the ribcage. Another way is to "flush" Spleen meridian by tracing it backwards once and then tracing it forwards three times. It can be done on both sides of the body at once.

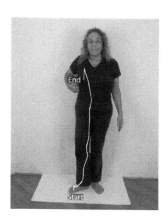

Chapter 10
Depression/Grief

Many things contribute to feelings of depression. Short-term depression can be related to health issues, environmental factors, social and/or relationship stress, sleep disturbances, or poor nutrition. When depression becomes chronic, it is not to be taken lightly, and it's advisable to seek the care of a physician. Energy techniques are a wonderful complement to other modalities including antidepressant medication.

I can remember how sad I was when I was not myself, watching from the sidelines, unable to live my usual life. It seemed like a normal reaction to my physical condition, but I was despondent and hopeless. I was grieving the loss of the me that used to be, and I didn't know if I would ever come back to "normal."

Here's something that helped me:

Place your hands over the center of your sternum and breath slowly and deeply into the **"Sea of Tranquility" CV 17** for two

minutes. This also activates your thymus. The bonus is more energy and a stronger immune system.

Often when we are depressed, we do shallow breathing, depriv-
ing ourselves of sufficient oxygen. Deep breathing brings in
oxygen and helps with letting go of waste products. Holding the
thumb and index finger together helps with letting go. The
thumb is the end point for Lung meridian; the index finger is the
beginning of Large Intestine meridian. Both are organs of elimination and of letting go. As you breath, imagine letting go of
past hurts and old baggage.

"**Letting Go**" (**Lu 1**) points on the soft area on either side of the upper chest are the beginning of Lung meridian. Press into these points, deeply inhale, and slowly release the pressure. Let your hands go outward and up; inhale and lift your chest; hold your breath. Release and allow your focus to be on your breath. Repeat as desired. Increasing the body's ability to breath deeply and assimilate oxygen counteracts feelings of depression.

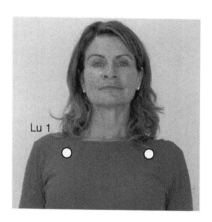

"**Heaven Rushing In**," by Donna Eden, is a good follow-up to the above. It's best to do it outside and barefoot but anywhere is good.

1. Rub your hands together and bring them to your thighs. Imagine the energy going through your legs into the ground.

2. Bring your hands together in front of your heart. Take a deep breath, open your arms to the sky, and let the energy pour into your heart space.

3. Hold your hand there as long as you need to. When you've had what you need, bring your hands to your heart and soak in the feelings from above.

Another exercise involves holding areas on the head while thinking a depressing thought. It sounds counter-intuitive, but placing one hand on the forehead and the other on the top of the head while concentrating on a thought you want to let go of helps shift the blood flow to the forebrain and allows the mind to clear a bit.

If you are feeling low and are someone who loves visualizing, here's a great way to spend a few minutes. By the time I've finished this visualization, my mood has shifted, I am feeling some joy, and life looks a little less gloomy.

1. Relax in a chair, and surround yourself in a color you love. Spend about thirty seconds covered in the hue of the moment.

2. Think of someone or something that makes you feel happy. Hold that in your mind for another thirty seconds.

3. Visualize someone or something you are grateful for. This time, spend about a minute feeling and sending gratitude.

Stretching Lung and Large Intestine meridians is a great way to clear stagnant emotional energy. Both meridians are associated with grief and sadness and run between the thumb and index fingers, and the chest and face.

1. Stand with your legs about hip-distance apart.

2. Clasp your hands behind your back and slowly bend forward at the waist; at the same time, raise your clasped hands over your head. Enjoy this stretch for at least thirty seconds. Notice the stretch in your upper back and chest. You are also releasing points along the

Bladder meridian, stimulating emotional balancing points, good for insomnia and depression.

3. Slowly release your arms back to your sides.

4. Bend your knees and use your thighs as you slowly come back to a standing position.

Another help for depression is getting your brain to crossover. Our brains are meant to naturally crossover, sending information from the left hemisphere to the right side of the body, and the right hemisphere to the left side of the body. When the brain doesn't communicate correctly, activities—and life in general— are much more difficult. The brain is not working at full-capacity, and healing takes longer.

When we have been depressed or have a chronic illness, our activities decrease, and we have less opportunity to walk naturally and swing our arms. We might be carrying a bag or briefcase, keep our hands in our pockets, or just keep our arms still; all these activities prevent the energy in our brain from crossing over, inhibiting the crossover pattern.

One simple technique I like can be done anywhere and involves making an X over the torso by taking one hand and putting it on the opposite shoulder; with some pressure drag your hand over the shoulder to the opposite hip. Now do the same thing with the other arm. Do at least five on each side of the body.

A more involved exercise is called Cross Crawl. This also helps the brain to crossover and can be done sitting or standing or, if you like, to music. Lift your right arm and your left leg at the same time. Then lift your right leg and your left arm. Continue this pattern, like an exaggerated march for about a minute.

Chapter 11
Facial Paralysis (Bell's Palsy)

One of the effects of Lyme can be facial paralysis.

I found this technique for facial paralysis in a book called *Tsubo* by Katsusuke Serizawa, MD. It may offer some relief for facial paralysis. As he states in the book, persevere because success cannot be expected in a day.

1. Massage the forehead by moving from the center of your forehead out to the temples.

2. Massage from the inner corner of the eye along the underside of the eyebrow to the depression at the outer end of the brow.

3. Massage from the center of the cheek to the front of the ear opening. Then massage to the depression behind the earlobe. Next massage from the center of the cheek down to the corner of the jaw.

4. Massage along the upper lip and bottom lip from the center to the corners of the mouth.

Doing figure eights over the face, especially where there is palsy, is a good tool for healing. Use figure eight patterns over any area whenever you have an injury or a pain.

Chapter 12
Fatigue/Fibromyalgia

Fibromyalgia is an elusive disease to diagnose and affects many humans causing much frustration and anxiety. The symptoms can be vague, which makes it hard to diagnose. Because so many of the symptoms are similar, fibromyalgia and Lyme can be challenging to differentiate at first. There is some mention in the literature of Lyme possibly triggering fibromyalgia and chronic fatigue syndrome (CFS). Fibromyalgia and CFS may be linked to stress, hormones, and chemical imbalances. Chronic fatigue is also believed to be a viral infection due to a weakened immune system.

There is a connection between trauma and stress, which affects the hypothalamus-pituitary-adrenal axes. It has been stated that some folks don't display Lyme symptoms until there is a major stressor in their lives, triggering that hypothalamus-pituitary-adrenal connection and causing the appearance of Lyme symptoms.

Immune system abnormalities can cause exhaustion and muscle pain. Both can cause the onset of viral infections, retroviruses, and excess yeast in the system. Antibiotics, steroids, thyroid medicine, chemical toxins, oral contraceptives, and heredity can exacerbate challenges to the immune system. The immune system acts like it is constantly under attack. This is when Triple Warmer is working overtime to keep you well.

Triple Warmer is the meridian related to the fight, flight, or freeze reaction in the body and helps us when things we experience are out of the norm. Most of us live in a world where our Triple Warmer is often triggered. Here are a few exercises I learned from Donna Eden to calm that meridian. Donna calls this one the Triple Warmer Smoothie.

Triple Warmer Smoothie

1. Place your fingers at your temples. Hold for one deep breath, breathing in through your nose and out through your mouth.

2. On another deep in-breath, slowly slide your fingers up and around your ears with some pressure.

3. As you exhale, slide your fingers down and behind your ears, press them down the sides of your neck, and hang them on your shoulders.

4. Push your fingers into your shoulders and smooth them to the middle of your chest, with one arm resting on top of the other.

5. Hold there for several deep breaths.

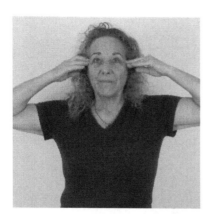 

This is another one of my favorites since it can be done anywhere without folks noticing you are calming yourself. It calms Triple Warmer and strengthens Spleen at the same time, supporting your immune system. When you reverse your hold, you will be calming Triple Warmer and sending energy to your Liver.

Nurturing Hug

1. Wrap your left hand around your right arm, just above the elbow.

2. Wrap your right arm around the left side of your body, underneath your breast.

3. Hold this position for at least three deep breaths.

4. Reverse sides.

Dietary suggestions

Dietary ideas to help with fibromyalgia include decreasing or eliminating dairy as it causes congestion; decrease cold or raw foods as they strain the system, especially in cold weather; increase greens as they increase vitality and boost immunity; eat sea vegetables for their trace minerals; reduce wheat and yeast; eliminate sugar; eat fruit in moderation; eliminate caffeine, soda, and alcohol. It is important to get enough protein.

Other suggestions include sleeping with your head to the north. Soaking your feet and massaging your toes can help as well. If you like to take baths, here's a formula that will relieve stiffness and revitalize the digestive system:

1. Freshly grate one-quarter cup of ginger root.

2. Place the ginger in cheesecloth and make a giant teabag.

3. Place this "teabag" in your bathtub while you lounge for fifteen minutes.

It is essential to oxygenate the body since fatigue is caused by an oxygen deficiency in the cells that is taxing the body. Brain fatigue affects the supraspinatus, a small muscle that sits on top of the shoulder blade on the upper back that is governed by Central Meridian, also known as Conception Vessel. You can help the supraspinatus by rubbing the area on both sides in front of the shoulder joint along the outside of your chest.

Points that help with fatigue and fibromyalgia

You can do one or all; start with light pressure and increase as you are able.

- **LI 11 "Pool at the Corner"** is found at the outer elbow crease and can help to fortify the immune system. Hold each side for two minutes. If you are able, you can cross your arms and hold both points at once.

- **LI 4 "Merging Valley"** can be found in the webbing between the thumb and index fingers. Holding these points firmly can be helpful with pain, inflammation, food sensitives, sluggish digestive system, and headaches.

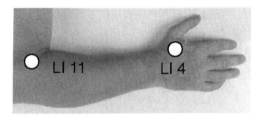

- **ST 36 "Three Mile Point"** is located about four finger-widths below the knee outside of the shin and helps with fatigue, endurance, and digestion. Press firmly for two minutes. You can rub it briskly when you feel fatigued and need a quick rush of energy.

- Breathing while firmly holding the tip of the index finger can help you relax. Hold your finger and breathe for two minutes.

- A great way to relieve stress and tension in the body is to hold the third eye point with **CV 17 "Sea of Tranquility"** in the center of the breastbone. Hold and breathe deeply for one to three minutes.

- To revitalize the entire body, rub your palms gently but firmly on your lower back at waist level. If that is too painful, just hold your back. You are stimulating an area known as **"Sea of Vitality."** Holding or rubbing that area also awakens a point called Ming Men, which is found behind the navel on the spine. This point has been referred to as our fountain of youth. It is on the Governing Vessel and clears heat from the body. It's good for tonifying the Kidneys, low back pain, adrenal exhaustion, and fatigue and a lot of other situations. I continue to be in awe of the power of the Ming Men point.

- **K 7 "Recover Flow"** is helpful to spark the energy systems of the body, especially the immune system. It's found in a natural depression between the Achilles tendon and the leg bone, about two inches above **K 3.**

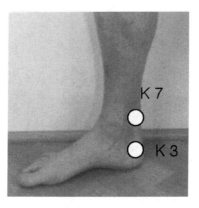

- **CV 6 "Sea of Energy"** is located about two inches below the belly button. Massaging it in small circular movements "sparks" energy flow, adds fire to the system, supports digestion and healthy bowels. (Avoid using when there are flare-ups and widespread inflammation.)

- **Lu 9 "Great Abyss"** is found on the wrist crease along the thumb-side of the hand. Massage it slowly with circular clockwise movements to enhance immune function; it helps to build and support the flow of qi. This point helps to break through the stagnation characteristic of chronic fatigue syndrome.

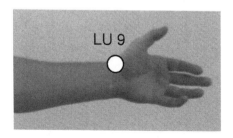

Chapter 13
Fear

So much of what I remember about my early days of Lyme is how fearful I was that I would never walk again, and that I wouldn't be able to recover and do all the things that I previously had been able to do. Thankfully, there are easy ways to move out of fear.

One is to hold one hand on the forehead and the other at the back of the head. This is called a frontal/occipital hold. While you take some slow breaths, focus on your fear. Hold this until your feel pulsing in the palm on your forehead or you are having a difficult time continuing to hold onto the fearful thought.

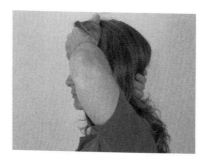

Fear stimulates the adrenals, which produce adrenaline, and the fight-or-flight response. Adrenaline also stimulates the Kidneys.

Strengthening the Kidneys can help to balance fears. One simple way to nourish and strengthen the Kidneys is by twisting the torso. You can find twisting exercises in yoga and chi gong, or you can try this simple twist: stand with your feet hip distance apart and swing your arms so that you twist your torso and lightly slap your lower back.

Some points to use

- **CV 17 "Sea of Tranquility,"** located in the center of the breastbone, can calm a panic or anxiety attack, open your chest and ease your breathing.

- **K 27 "Elegant Mansion"** clears your throat, counteracts fear, and calms you. This last point on the Kidney meridian is found below the corners of your collarbone.

- **CV 6 "Sea of Qi"** is about three finger-widths below your navel. To get rid of old fears, hold this point while breathing slowly and deeply and know you have the courage to face old fears.

- **GB 14 "Yang White"** can help reprogram fearful thoughts and clear the mind. Hold this point for one minute by lightly placing your middle fingers on your forehead about one finger-width above your eyebrow in line with your pupil.

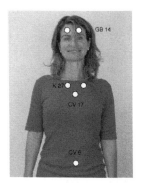

- To stop excessive fear, squeeze behind the anklebone on the inside and outside of your foot. Hold for one minute on your right foot and then hold for one minute on the left. These points, **K 6 "Shining Sea"** and **B 62 "Extending Vessel,"** are valuable to use with phobias.

- **St 36** is such a great point to get energy flowing and strengthen the entire body. It's also great to counteract fears and phobias. Rub briskly with your fists up and down your outer shinbone for one minute.

Chapter 14
Headaches

Headaches are familiar to most of us. They can vary in intensity and cause. They can also be signals to the body. One signal may be that the brain isn't getting enough oxygen. In TCM, it can indicate that there is "heat" in the body.

If there are stress and tight shoulder muscles, massaging around the base of the head and neck can be helpful. Sometimes tight neck muscles can be related to sinuses and the body's immune response. Headaches can also be related to a disruption in the flow of nutrients from the small intestine to the large intestine that affects the process of eliminating waste. Sometimes digestion of fats can cause toxicity, producing what are known as Gall Bladder headaches. Overloading the Liver, our body's filter for all the blood that enters the digestive track, can cause long-lasting headaches.

Here are some tips for an assortment of headache types:

Massaging the fingers and toes can help relieve a headache. When it is in the front of the head, massage the second and third toes. If the headache is felt in the back or side of the head, massage the fourth and fifth toes. Headaches that feel like they are coming from inside the head respond to deep massage of the thumbs, middle, ring, and little finger. Doing this two or three times a day can help.

The following points are for headaches and migraines. I learned many of these effective points when I was studying Shiatsu and called them "headache points." They were held with strong pressure for ten seconds at each location three times. The easiest way to work these points is to place your thumbs in the spot(s) and tilt your head back over your fingers and breathe. These points will also help with tension in the shoulders and neck, sinus congestion, and eyestrain.

- **GV 16 "Wind Mansion"** is found in the hollow at the base of the skull.

- **BL 10 "Pillar of Heaven"** is on either side of GV 16, about two finger-widths away.

- **GB 20 "Gates of Consciousness"** is located at the base of the skull in a hollow between the neck muscles.

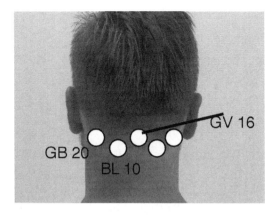

- **BL 2 "Drilling Bamboo"** is located in the indentations where the eyebrow meets the bridge of the nose. This helps with sinus and eye pain. Hold for one to two minutes.

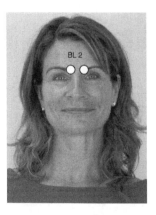

- **LI 4 "Joining the Valley,"** found in the webbing between the thumb and index finger, relieves headaches that are sensed in the front of the head.

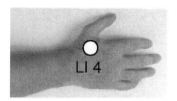

- **LV 3 "Bigger Rushing"** is on the top of the foot in the hollow between the big toe and second toe. This is an important Liver point and is helpful with headaches, eyestrain, hangovers, and clearing the Liver. I massage this point every day when I am putting on my socks.

- **GB 41 "Above Tears"** is a vital point along Gall Bladder meridian found on the top of the foot in the groove between the fourth and fifth toes about one inch up from the toes. This point helps with shoulder tension, migrating pain, water retention, as well as headaches.

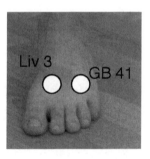

Donna Eden offers a technique she calls the "Headache Isometric Press," which helps with preventing headaches as well as resolving them.

Headache Isometric Press

1. Sitting in a relaxed position, tilt your head to the right with your ear close to your right shoulder.

2. Place your right palm against the side of your head and press your head into your palm as you press your palm against the side of your head. Hold your breath while you push hard.

3. Release your hand and allow your head to go closer to your shoulder; repeat two more times.

4. Repeat all of the above on the left side.

Here's another way to help with tension headaches.

1. Massage the "headache points" (see above) along the base of the skull, rubbing firmly with circular motions.

2. Massage your neck, starting at the bottom, and with pressure, drag your fingers to the sides.

3. Repeat this massage, going up a little higher each time, until you get to the top of your neck.

For headaches arising from digestive issues and constipation, sometimes a stomach massage can help. Another technique to re-establish the smooth flow from the small to large intestine is re-setting the ileocecal valve.

1. Place your right hand on your right hip bone with your little finger on the inside edge of your hip.

2. Place your left hand on the left hip at the same spot.

3. With pressure, drag your fingers up about six inches, taking a deep inhale each time. Repeat four times.

4. End by dragging your thumbs down one time.

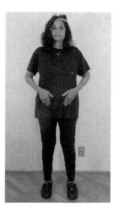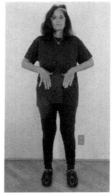

Chapter 15
Immune System and Spleen

Having a challenged immune system makes one vulnerable to infection and illness. In TCM, the immune system is governed by Kidney, Liver, Lung, and Spleen. A strong Spleen is essential to keeping the immune system strong.

The Spleen stores the blood and acts like a pump for the red blood cells that carry oxygen and the white blood cells that fight infection. The Spleen also destroys old blood cells and produces plasma cells. Spleen imbalances weaken the blood and Qi and make us more susceptible to disease. If Spleen is unable to get energy from food, Kidney is unable to generate the "fire" needed to spark our life force, and feed our ambition, drive, and willpower.

A great way to strengthen Spleen meridian is to do a Do-In exercise, which stretches both Earth element meridians - Spleen and Stomach.

1. Sit on the ground on your knees with arms clasped overhead.

2. Lower your body backwards towards the floor (eventually having the shoulders touching the floor) and take two deep breaths.

3. Change the position of your hands by having a different thumb on top. Take two deep breaths. Note if there is a difference between sides.

Our immune system tends to be strongest at about 7 a.m. (the beginning of Earth time on the Meridian clock). The immune system is responsive to our emotional states. If we are angry, antibodies increase. If we are relaxed, it can improve our immunity. Using guided imagery is another immune booster. The thymus, Spleen, lymph system, and bone marrow are important in activating the immune system.

- A wonderful way to stimulate the immune system is by tapping your thymus, which lies behind the sternum.

- Activating compassion for oneself is helpful. Massaging **H 8 "Little Palace"** can assist with that. It's found on the palm between the fourth and fifth fingers; when you make a fist, it can be found at the tip of the fifth finger. I like massaging this point between 11 a.m. and 1 p.m. when Heart meridian is at its most active.

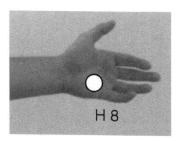

- Calming Triple Warmer by doing the Nurturing Hug is another way to strengthen Spleen and activate your immune system.

Stimulating the 'Strange Flows' helps to activate the immune system. Strange Flows, or Extraordinary Vessels in TCM, or Radiant Circuits from Eden Energy Medicine, are subtle energy flows that support the other energy systems, especially the meridians. They send energy where it is needed, are responsive to emotions, and produce joy and positivity.

One way you can do this is by doing an exercise I call Compassionate Hearts. While I trace the hearts, I repeat the affirmations found in italics. Some days, the words of compassion are for me; other days, I have others in mind when I say them.

Compassionate Hearts

1. With your hands on the front of your thighs, take a deep breath in and out.

2. Inhale and move your hands slowly up the front of your body to the top of your forehead. Exhale and trace a heart around your face from your forehead to your chin. (***Think love.***) Repeat two more times.

3. Take a deep breath as you move your hands slowly down to the middle of your chest to your heart chakra. Exhale. Inhale and with flattened hands, trace a heart going up over the chest, and while exhaling, finish the heart by moving your hands around the trunk of your body, down the inside of the hip bones, ending at the top of the pubic bone. (***Feel love.***) Repeat two more times, moving from the top of the pubic bone to the center of the chest on an inhale and complete the heart on an exhale.

4. With an inhale, trace a heart starting at your pubic bone, go up and over to the hips, and finish the heart going down the outside of the legs ending between your feet. (***Act with love.***) Repeat two more times.

5. Finally, as you inhale, draw your hands up your body from your feet to the top of your chest; bring your hands into a prayerful position and raise them above

your head. Separate your hands and lift them a bit; turn your palms outward, then slowly exhale, and with resistance, trace a heart around your body with outstretched arms. (***Spread love.***)

Chapter 16
Infection

Infection usually indicates that there are signs of Heat in the body. What does that mean? Heat is considered a yang condition, causing expansion and activity. It also indicates a system out of balance, manifesting with irritability, fever, inflammation, red skin, swelling, pain in the joints, and agitation. Heat tends to affect the body fluids leading to thirst, constipation, and dark urine.

Heat in the organs affects the emotions primarily. Heart Fire causes emotional disturbances, fidgeting, and insomnia. Heat in the Liver can stir extreme anger. Heat in the Stomach can lead to mouth ulcers and constipation. Heat in the Lungs can manifest as an accumulation of yellow mucus.

One method of dealing with Heat is to avoid foods and drugs that intensify the heat symptoms; these are sugar, coffee, spicy foods, alcohol, and amphetamines. Because Heat is related to Fire, another good way to cool the Heat is to drink water because Water balances Fire.

Spleen governs infections, so doing Spleen-strengthening exercises like Flush and Tap can help. To flush the Spleen meridian, trace it backwards one time and then forwards three times.

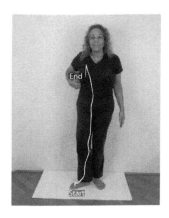

Chapter 17
Insomnia/Sleep Disturbances

There are several types of sleep disturbances. For some people, it's trouble getting to sleep. For others, it's waking frequently during the night and having trouble returning to sleep. Waking too early in the morning and feeling that sleep wasn't refreshing or it "wasn't enough" affects others.

Some of us are familiar with the discomfort of not getting enough sleep and the resistance to sleep when the mind won't shut off. The time when you most often awaken during the night can be informative. If it's between 11 p.m. and 1 a.m., massage the *neurolymphatic* points for Gall Bladder on both sides of the sternum between the third and fourth and fourth and fifth ribs. Feelings of repressed anger or a rich diet can interrupt sleep between 1 and 3 a.m.

Doing the Fists of Anger exercise will help to release the extra energy carried with the anger.

Massaging the neurolymphatic point for Liver on the right side of the body between the fifth and sixth ribs will aid in digestion of fats.

Waking between 3 and 5 a.m. can indicate grief or the need to let go. Holding the Lung *NV* point on the top of the head, along with the forehead, will help to calm those feelings.

For a peaceful sleep, we need to release all the day's tensions from physical activities and mental thoughts. To ensure a good night's sleep, it's important to deal with any disturbing emotions as well as exercise to stretch and open the meridians. Some quick and natural ways to fall asleep include yawning and stretching, slow, deep breathing, eye rotations with eyes open and closed, a hot bath, chamomile tea, gentle yoga, and deep relaxation. If you have a hard time falling asleep, check that your calcium and magnesium intake is sufficient. These nutrients can be found in dairy, egg yolks, green leafy vegetables, beans, nuts, strawberries, lemons, and oranges.

I have a few methods to lull myself back to sleep and one is paying gratitude to each of my body parts. Sometimes I thank muscles and structure; another time I pay tribute to my organs. I figure if I can't sleep and my mind wants to be busy, I might as well be busy with something positive for my health. Often I fall asleep only to reawaken wondering where I left off with my thanks. Most times I fall asleep with a peaceful and grateful mind.

Here are more things to do:

In TCM, insomnia is viewed as an imbalance between Fire and Water. One way to create balance is take at least three breaths while holding **H 7 "Gate of God"** and **K 3 "Great Brook"** on one side of the body at a time. **H 7** is found on the wrist crease along the line from your little finger, and **K 3** is located in the depression halfway between your Achilles tendon and your ankle bone on the inside of your foot..

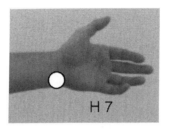

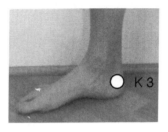

Another set of points to hold are **CV 6 "Ocean of Ki"** and **CV 17 "Middle of the Chest."** Hold them gently as you take three or more breaths. **CV 6** is about one and a half inch below your navel, and **CV 17** is in the center of the sternum.

To integrate your head and your belly, hold **CV 6 "Ocean of Ki"** (see above) and **GV 20 "Hundred Meeting,"** found on the top of your head on a line connecting the top of your ears, while taking deep breaths.

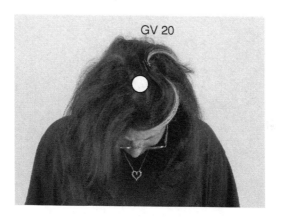

When insomnia is due to anxiety or over-excitement, hold **H 7** with a gentle, calm, and loving touch.

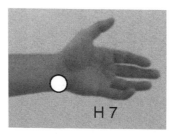

Another favorite I learned is to hold Triple Warmer neurovascular points found at the temple and the hollow in the throat. Use a three finger notch (thumb, index, and middle fingers together) at both locations and take five slow, deep breaths. Then switch hand positions so you are placing your fingers on the other temple and breathe as before. This calms Triple Warmer and helps put you back to sleep. If it doesn't work the first time, repeat as needed.

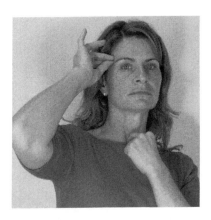

Chapter 18
Joint Inflammation

One major challenge of Lyme disease is aching joints, not unlike arthritis. When held for several minutes every day, the acupressure points offered can relieve muscle aches, increase mobility of achy joints, strengthen them, and prevent further deterioration of the joint.

- LI 4 "Joining the Valley" is found in the webbing between the thumb and index finger and can relieve pain and inflammation in the neck, shoulder, elbow, wrist, and hand.

- TW 5 "Outer Gate," found about two inches up from the wrist crease on the outer forearm, can be helpful with wrist and shoulder pain.

- LI 11 "Crooked Pond," located on the outside of the arm at the elbow crease, is helpful with wrist and shoulder pain.

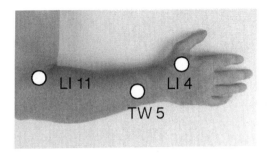

- **GB 20 "Gates of Consciousness"** relieves arthritis pain, headaches, stiff neck, and general irritability. Find it below the base of the skull, in the hollow behind the ears.

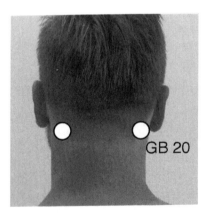

Chapter 19
Kidneys

We are born into this life with a certain amount of Kidney *jing* or life force. It is composed of congenital *jing a*nd acquired *jing*. As we age or are challenged by illness, our congenital Kidney energy depletes. Acquired *jing* comes from the food processed by Spleen and Stomach. The Kidney meridian is the foundation for the body's yin and yang. It is often referred to as the "pilot light" for the body, so keeping it glowing and strong is essential. Kidney energy is important for many things like creating bone marrow, development of the brain, bone health, water metabolism and the fluids in the body, and the function of our ears. They house our willpower and determination and support our memory.

It is essential, in my view, to support Kidney. One way is to strengthen the meridian by tracing the Kidney meridian forward. Sometimes though, the meridian is unable to take in the energy because it is so depleted. Those times, it's necessary to calm or sedate the meridian first before strengthening it. I like to compare it with a garden hose that has a clog. No matter how much water you try to push through it, the water won't flow. You must clear the clog before water will flow through the hose. Well, that's what calming or sedating the meridian before strengthening it is like. I have used this technique often on myself and in my Energy Medicine practice.

One way to strengthen Kidney meridian is to do an exercise called Kidney Flush. This can be done by tracing Kidney meridian backwards once and then forward three times. Kidney meridian starts under the ball of each foot, travels up the inside of the foot, circles around the ankle, and goes straight up the body and ends at the corners of the collarbones.

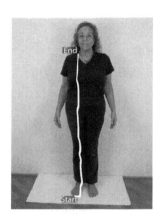

Chapter 20
Liver

The liver is a hardworking organ, filtering toxins and waste products from the blood and producing chemicals that break down fats among many other things. In Traditional Chinese Medicine, the Liver controls the healthy flow of blood and qi to every cell of the body. When Liver qi is constrained or exhausted from stress, poor diet, and lack of sleep and exercise, toxins build up in the blood and vital energy slows. This can lead to chronic irritability and overreacting emotionally and a cycle with more anxiety, fear, anger and over-excitement.

There are many dietary guidelines to help your Liver create a smooth flow of energy:

- Restrict your fat intake, especially from animal products and tropical oils and "partially hydrogenated" oils found in many prepared foods, fast foods, and pastries.

- Reduce your intake of caffeine and soft drinks.

- Avoid highly processed and refined foods.

- Eat organic foods whenever possible.

- Increase your intake of raw whole foods like fruits and vegetables.

- Drink eight to ten glasses of fresh filtered water daily

- Avoid alcohol, smoking, and illicit drugs.

Anger is very detrimental to the Liver. It has been said the eyes and the emotion of anger stimulate the muscles and liver and the flow of qi. Anger in the Liver can be mended with kindness for oneself and others. Consider doing the Compassionate Hearts exercise to bring kindness to self. Using your mind, see your Liver in your imagination. Draw in kindness as you inhale, release anger as you exhale.

Another method of healing the Liver is to inhale the color forest green and exhale what is no longer needed. Repeat each cycle five times. The Liver thrives on the color green.

Sour foods help the Liver because they are astringent and absorbent. They can also help with diarrhea or excess perspiring. Sour foods serve as a purifier and are crucial to clearing and cleaning Liver excess. A popular way to do a Liver cleanse uses lemon juice and olive oil and can be found in Jason Elias and Katherine Ketcham's book, *Chinese Medicine for Maximum Immunity*. It's my go-to book for my Spring cleanse — the season of the Liver.

Here are a few exercises to help the Liver:

A Do-In exercise for both the Liver and Gall Bladder involves sitting with both legs extended and opened as wide as possible into a V. With both hands, reach as far as possible towards one foot, keeping the knees down. Once at your maximum stretch, take two slow breaths and then raise your body. Then bend toward the other foot, repeating the same breathing. Notice any difference between sides as you stretch. Any difficulties indicates more stagnation in that side of the body.

Deeply massaging **LV 3 "Great Rush"** is a great way to keep your Liver clear. It is found in the notch between the big toe and second toe on top of the foot.

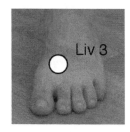

Chapter 21
Memory/Cognitive Challenges

Lyme disease is a disease of the white matter in the brain. It affects memory associations creating slowness of recall and incorrect associations. I've heard the term "brain fog" used to describe many conditions. The ability to pay attention can also show impairment.

People with chronic Lyme or the after effects can experience hyper-acuity of the senses with auditory being the most common. Sounds may seem louder and more annoying. Some people are affected by bright lights and others by artificial lights. Tactile hyper-acuity can be manifested as clothing feeling scratchy or tight-feeling or touch being painful. Olfactory responses include excessive reactions to smells, perfumes, soaps, and petroleum products.

Working memory issues, like forgetting where things are or where the car is parked, are not uncommon. Other challenges are memory encoding with improperly stored information or in inability to retrieve things in memory. With short-term memory, there may be a slowness of recall of factual information, the retrieval of letters or numbers in a sequence, letter reversals, improper spelling, and word substitutions. This process can feel like acquired dyslexia or learning disabilities. Imagery functions can also be challenged with intrusive images, nightmares, illusions, hallucinations, and depersonalization.

Central meridian is related to brain functions, like doing things automatically while doing other things and multitasking. Doing **Zip Up** and **Hook Up** will help to strengthen that meridian.

Zip Up by placing your hand at the bottom end of the Central meridian, at your pubic bone. Take a deep breath in as you move your hand straight up the center of your body to your lower lip. Repeat three times.

To Hook Up, put one finger in your navel and the other at the third eye and pull up at both spots while taking several breaths.

In Qi Gong theory, Kidney (fear) and adrenals (stress) reduce memory and create learning challenges. Holding your head with one hand on the base of your skull and the other on your forehead as you think of the stressful emotions one by one can help with balancing Kidney meridian and ease the stress.

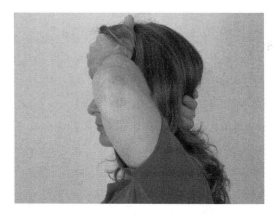

Here's an Eden technique that helps to keep memory sharp and to pump cerebral spinal fluid up the spine into the brain. It's called **Memory Breath.**

Memory Breath

- Place your left hand over your heart and your right palm on the right side of your head above your ear with your fingers pointed to the top of your head. Take four deep breaths.

- Move your right hand to the back of your head and do the same breathing.

- Place your right hand over your heart and your left hand over your ear; repeat the breathing.

- Place the palm of your left hand on your forehead with your fingers going to the top of your head and use the same breathing pattern.

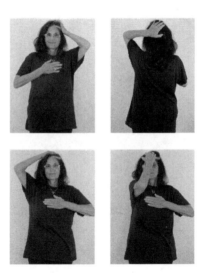

GV 26 "Center of the Person" also helps with memory, confusion, and concentration. It takes a firm pressure for two minutes above the upper lip, two-thirds of the way to the nose.

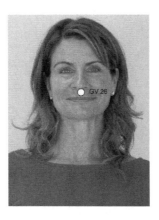

Here's a brain exercise that will unscramble your mind and is wonderful when there is confusion or overwhelm, disorganization, depression, excessive anger, or dyslexia:

- Sit in a chair with your back straight.

- Place your right foot over your left knee. Wrap your left hand around your right ankle and your right hand around the ball of your right foot.

- Breathe in slowly through your nose, letting the breath lift your body as you breathe in. At the same time, pull your leg toward you, creating a stretch. As you exhale, breathe out of your mouth slowly, letting your body relax. Repeat this four or five times.

- Switch to the other foot. Place your left foot over your right knee. Wrap your right hand around your left ankle and your left hand around the ball of your left foot. Use the same breathing as you repeat four or five times.

- Uncross your legs and place your fingertips together forming a pyramid. Bring your thumbs to rest on your third eye, just above the bridge of your nose. Breathe slowly in through your nose. Then breathe out through your mouth, allowing your thumbs to separate slowly across your forehead, pulling the skin.

There is another point on the body specifically for brain function. It's **GB 39** "**Suspended Bell**." It's located three thumb-widths above the ankle bone on the outside of the leg between the tendons. This point can be pointed at from one inch away for one minute.

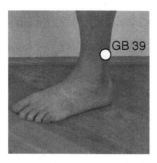

Another great exercise to enhance neurological organization of the brain is **Cross Crawl**. The left hemisphere of the brain sends information to the right side of the body, and the right hemisphere sends information to the left side of the body. We naturally perform the Cross Crawl activity when we walk or run. Often times when we are exhausted, have a chronic illness, depression, or are very stressed, the energy in our brain doesn't adequately cross over. Then our brain and our body will not be functioning at full capacity. When the energy stops crossing over, it's referred to as a homolateral pattern. Here are the exercises for Cross Crawl and **Homolateral Cross Crawl**:

Cross Crawl

Cross Crawl is similar to an exaggerated march while standing in place. Lift your right leg and tap your left hand to your knee and then lift the left leg and tap your knee with the right hand. This exercise can also be done while sitting. Continue this for about 30 seconds.

Homolateral Cross Crawl

Homolateral Cross Crawl can be done seated or standing and is helpful to keep your energies crossing over and with brain organization.

1. Raise the right foot and swing the right arm forward and begin marching in place for ten lifts, making sure that the pattern created is using the same arm and same leg. Stop and take a breath.

2. Raise the right foot and swing the left arm forward and begin marching in place for ten lifts, making sure that the pattern created is using the opposite arm to opposite leg. Stop and breathe.

3. Repeat step 1.

4. Repeat step 2.

5. Repeat step 2 one last time.

Chapter 22
Metabolism

Some folks have reported that their metabolism slows down with Lyme. Two meridians come to mind when I think about metabolism: Triple Warmer and Spleen. Triple Warmer because it governs the thyroid and gets surplus energy from Spleen. Sedating Triple Warmer and strengthening Spleen are ideals. Here are a few easy ways to do that:

Nurturing Hug

1. Wrap your left hand around your right arm, just above the elbow, a Triple Warmer point.

2. Wrap your right arm around the left side of your body, underneath your breast, where your Spleen sits.

3. Hold this position for at least three deep breaths.

4. Reverse sides, and you'll be strengthening Liver and calming Triple Warmer.

Tapping on Triple Warmer

This is a simple and great way to use when you are anxious and need calming. Place one hand on your heart and use the other hand to tap on the area between your ring and little finger. Breathe deeply as you tap about 10 times. Take a breath and tap again for about 30 times. Repeat with the other hand on your heart.

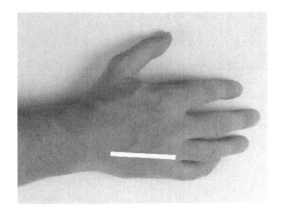

A great exercise for Thyroid, as well as balancing Triple Warmer, is to stretch your neck by placing your middle fingers on either side of your Adam's apple and stretching horizontally, vertically, and diagonally.

Oxygen is essential for metabolism and brain function. Having good blood attracts oxygen to the body through good food like green leaves. The chlorophyll found in green leafy vegetables helps the body to create red blood cells, the carriers of oxygen. They also help with clearer thinking as the body needs oxygen for the brain to function at its best.

Spleen strengthening is another way to boost metabolism since that is the role of both the Spleen meridian and the organ. One way is to trace the meridian backward one time and forward three times, ending with vigorous tapping of the Spleen NV point.

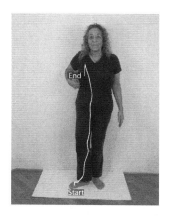

Chapter 23
Muscles

Muscles, ligaments, and tendons—the body parts that provide us with strength and flexibility—are governed by Liver and Wood element. Muscle fatigue or weakness may be due to an imbalance in Wood or Liver meridian. The neurolymphatic area for Liver and Wood element is found on your right side between the fifth and sixth ribs, from the nipple to the sternum. Rubbing there will help with muscle aches. There will probably be tenderness at first. The more you rub the area, the less tender it will be and the less achy your muscles will be.

Some texts say that Earth rules muscles, so when there is pain or stiffness, check the Stomach and Spleen neurolymphatic points, which are found under the left breast. Luckily, those areas can be addressed at the same time by firmly massaging in small circles.

Chapter 24
Neurotic Behavior

Our brain and nervous system are like electrical wiring. And like electrical wiring, our nervous system needs to be grounded. Any shocks to our system should travel through Bladder meridian from our heads down through our toes into the earth. Many things can get in the way of that happening: stress can get stuck in the body circling around and not exiting into earth, or meridian points can be overcharged, causing our "circuit breakers" to show imbalance.

It is said that a disturbance in Kidney, Bladder meridian's yin partner, can be a direct cause of melancholy, hysteria, and neuroses. A recommendation from *Healing Ourselves* is to stimulate Kidney qi with onions, garlic, hot peppers, scallions, ginger, and shiso leaves.

In TCM, it's believed that neurotic behavior is caused by an excess of Metal element, which is associated with Lung and Large Intestine meridians.

Neuroses, it's said, are often caused by long periods of mental conflict or stress, or a stressful diet. This can cause an imbalance in Liver energy.

Neurotic feelings can manifest as being easily tired or fatigued, having insomnia, waking early easily, a state of dreaminess, destructibility, bad memory, hypersensitivity to sound, smell, or light, palpitations, belching and distended stomach, constipation, or anorexia.

A point to hold to get your Liver moving is **Liv 3 "Great Rushing."**

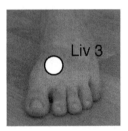

The value of using the Energy Psychology technique of tapping on acupressure points for emotional discomfort cannot be understated. See pages 29 & 30 for tapping points.

Chapter 25
Numbness (Emotional)

Many folks I've spoken with about Lyme disease say they've experienced trauma and PTSD from the painful experiences of misdiagnosis, ineffective treatment, prolonged healing, the inability to continue to work, being on disability, and bankruptcy. One adaptive response to trauma is to shut down and become emotionally numb.

There are ways to deal with the emotional numbness left by trauma, and they fall in the Energy Psychology category. Often referred to as Tapping, Thought Field Therapy (TFT), or Emotional Freedom Technique (EFT), each offers an effective method of dealing with trauma. I believe it's best to work with a clinician skilled in energy psychology techniques who can teach you how to do it for yourself.

See pages 29 & 30 for tapping points.

Chapter 26
Pain

One of my vivid memories of Lyme disease was the excruciating pain that seemed unrelenting. At times there was no comfortable spot except the tub filled with warm water, and I am normally not a fan of baths. Then when I could no longer lift my leg to get into the water, that place of relief also was gone. Thankfully, when I got my mind working again, I was able to use some of the techniques listed below.

In TCM, pain is considered a signal that there is an abundance of energy, often stagnated, in that area. Stress can cause a neuro-muscular imbalance resulting in a flare up and increased pain. The more tense you are, the more the awareness of pain. Relaxation brings with it an increased flow of energy and promotes healing. So when there is pain, moving the energy is the goal.

Acupressure can block pain signals by releasing endorphins, the neurochemicals that reduce pain, with no side effects.

Try using the following points:

- **LI 4 "Merging Valley"** is helpful with shoulder pain and headaches; **GB 20 "Wind Pool"** relieves headaches and neck stiffness and irritability.

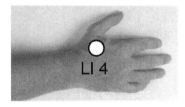 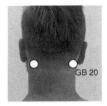

- **K 3 "Great Stream"** helps with swollen feet and ankle pain and is found behind the ankle bone on the inside of the leg; **Bl 60 "Name of the Mountains"** is good for sciatica and is found on the outside of the ankle bone. Held together, they are wonderful for back pain.

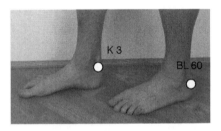

Energy psychology has some tapping protocols for pain.

See pages 29 & 30 for tapping points.

Chapter 27
PTSD/Trauma

The experience of a debilitating disease can be traumatic, both emotionally and physically. In my own case, one trauma happened when I fell to the ground while using my walker in a public venue. The inability to walk upstairs and feeling totally incapacitated were other traumatic situations, as were watching my garden die because I couldn't tend it and not being able to do things for myself.

Trauma leaves an imprint on our muscles as well as our emotions. One reason massage or bodywork is so essential to healing is that unless the feelings are released from the muscles, ailments and problems continue. To heal from an emotional wound, one must explore the painful and challenging memories and feelings. Acupressure has been found to be helpful in the discovery and release of past traumas. Evidence exists that holding acupressure points for several minutes releases endorphins, the body's neurochemicals that help alleviate pain, and increases circulation. Holding the points can allow space for the traumatic memories to be released.

Here are some quick things to do for PTSD and trauma:

- Give yourself a foot massage if you are able. It can be as brief as two minutes. If you have someone in your life that will help you, ask them to massage your feet.

- Pressing on **CV 17 "Sea of Tranquility"** (on your breastbone at the level of your heart) for two minutes while breathing slowly can help to calm a panic attack and allow for deeper, calmer breathing as the grip of panic releases.

- Sometimes disorientation and disassociation occur after a trauma. Rubbing the outside of the lower leg along the shinbone for one minute can help with disorientation as well as dizziness, palpitations, and anxiety.

- Pressing into your palm on a point known as **P 8** "**Palace of Toil**" with the thumb or middle finger of the opposing hand can bring balance to the mind and spirit following trauma. Hold the point on both sides for maximum benefit.

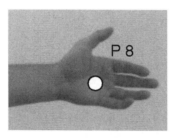

- There are points on both sides of your forehead, about a finger-width above the eyebrows in line with the center of the eyeball, which can reprogram your thought patterns, calm your mind, and clear away the fear from trauma. All it takes is a gentle touch on **GB 14 "Yang White."**

- Stretching is another great thing to do to release the muscle contractions and stiffness that often accompany traumatic memories. Take five to ten minutes to do some gentle stretching, increasing circulation, flexibility, and tone.

A wonderful point to aid in "**Letting Go**" is **Lu 1**. It's located bilaterally on the upper part of the chest, near where the shoulder and chest meet.

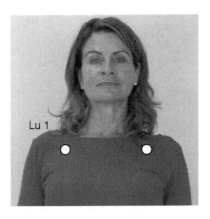

A great stretch I learned from Donna Eden, which she calls "**Connecting Heaven and Earth**," creates space in the joints and releases excess energy:

1. Rub your hands together briskly and place your hands on your thighs, fingers spread. Feel the energy moving towards your feet, grounding you.

2. Deeply inhale through the nose. Circle your arms out and have your hands meet mid-chest in prayer position; exhale through the mouth.

3. Inhale, stretch one hand straight up, the other straight down; flatten your hands, fingers pointing away from the body, one pushing up to sky, the other pushing down to earth. Hold.

4. Exhale; return hands to prayer position. Repeat, switching arms.

5. Release pose; fold body over at the waist. Hang there, knees slightly bent for two breaths.

6. Return to standing slowly; as you do, make figure eights with your hands up your body to your head. Let the energy roll down your back.

Another great technique for dealing with panic is to hold your forehead and the bulge at the back of your head while thinking about what is causing your feelings. This might be done in the presence of another person, especially if the trauma is over-whelming.

There are wonderful methods to deal with panic and trauma using energy psychology. As stated previously, please seek the assistance of a qualified psychotherapist if the trauma is severe.

See pages 29 & 30 for tapping points.

Chapter 28
Stomachaches, Indigestion

For some folks, digestion can be challenged by Lyme. Here are some tips to help with indigestion:

- Reduce stomach acidity by avoiding acidic foods.

- Avoid eating cold foods or drinking cold water with meals.

- Relax before and during eating.

- Eat slowly; chew thoroughly.

- Try fasting or go on an elimination diet to see what foods trigger your discomfort.

Here are some points that can assist if you suffer from stomach troubles:

- **CV 12 "Central of Power"** is a great point for relieving and preventing indigestion. This is best to do on an empty stomach. Avoid if there is serious illness, heart issues, cancer, or high blood pressure. For best results, hold this point for no longer than two minutes. It's found in the center of the body, halfway between the bottom of the sternum and the navel.

- **CV 6 "Sea of Energy,"** found two finger-widths below the belly button, relieves pain, gas, constipation, and digestive problems.

- **St 36 "Three Mile Point"** relieves fatigue, poor digestion, and stomachaches. Find it on the outside of the shinbone, four finger-widths below the knee.

- **ST 25 "Hinge of the Heaven"** is also helpful with stagnation in the stomach, constipation, and diarrhea. It is located two finger-widths on either side of the navel. Be gentle with this point, and hold for a minute or two.

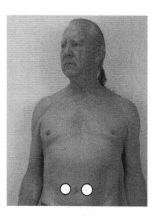

- **P 6 "Inner Gate"** sits in the middle of the inner arm, about two and a half finger-widths above the wrist. It helps with indigestion, nausea, and anxiety, as well as stomachaches.

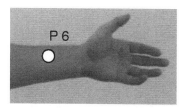

- **Sp 4** "**Grandfather Grandson**" relieves cramps, stomachaches, indigestion, and diarrhea. It's found on the arch about one thumb-width from the ball of the foot toward the heel.

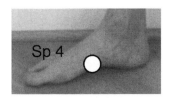

A wonderful pose I learned from yoga is called "**Gas-Relieving Pose.**" It's easy and involves lying on your back and bringing your legs, one at a time, to your chest. Hug your leg to you as you take a few deep breaths for about thirty seconds. Then switch legs. You can repeat this several times. You can also hug both legs to your chest if you are able. Hold this pose with eyes closed, taking slow breaths for at least a minute. Relax, you just might expel excess gas.

Another thing you can do to alleviate stomach pain is trace Stomach meridian backwards. To go backwards on the meridian, start at the second toe, go up the leg on the outside of the shin, up to the front of the hip, come in towards the side of the navel, and go up to the collarbone. Come up the front of the neck to the jaw, straight up to above the eye, around towards the eye, and end in the center of the cheek.

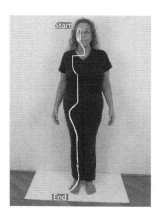

Rubbing firmly under the left breast, between the fifth and sixth ribs helps with digestion.

Also helpful for emotional stomach distress are points found on the bulge of the forehead between the eyebrows and the hairline. Hold these for a few minutes until you feel calm.

Chapter 29
Thyroid

The function of the thyroid is to balance the metabolism in the breaking down or regeneration of tissues. It also balances body temperature and fat content of the body. It is governed by Triple Warmer meridian and is related to Teres Minor, a shoulder muscle.

A way to balance Triple Warmer along with the thyroid is to use neurovascular reflex points. Place your thumbs, index, and middle fingers together, and gently place the fingertips of one hand at your temple. Place the fingertips of the other hand gently in the hollow at the base of your throat. Take four or five slow, deep breaths, and then change to hold the other temple along with the throat hollow.

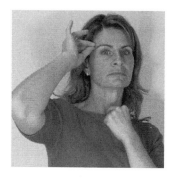

Healthy adrenals are essential for optimal thyroid function. Notice if you have salt cravings. That can indicate adrenal fatigue. Exhaustion, from things like sleep difficulties, illness, or pain, can cause adrenal insufficiency which in turn can affect the production of thyroid hormone uptake. Hypothyroidism can occur if the thyroid is not functioning properly, it is producing reduced levels of hormones, or the body isn't using the hormones effectively.

One way to bring energy to the thyroid is to stretch your throat. Donna Eden suggests placing your middle fingers above and below your Adam's apple. Stretch the skin on your neck horizontally, vertically, and diagonally.

The thyroid also affects the condition of the skin. Gach offers these points for balancing the thyroid and creating skin that has a glow:

- **TW 17 "Wind Screen"** and **SI 17 "Heavenly Appearance"** points are located behind the ear. **TW 17** is in the indentation directly behind the earlobe, and SI 17 is directly below that and behind the jawbone. Use your index and middle fingers to press into these tender points for one minute.

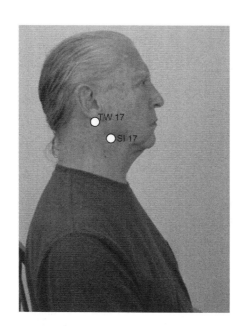

Chapter 30
Water Retention

Some people suffering from Lyme have mentioned feeling bloated. Edema, or fluid retention, can be from medication side-effects, illness, poor lymphatic drainage, a sedentary lifestyle, or too much salty food. In Chinese Medicine, it is associated with a weakness in Spleen and Kidney meridians. Points to help with relieving edema are:

- Sp 9 "Yin Mound Spring," found in a hollow on the inside of the lower leg right below the knee, will also help with knee pain.

- Sp 6 "Three Yin Intersection" is a point on the inner leg about four finger-widths above the anklebone. This is a versatile and important point. It's where three meridians — Kidney, Spleen and Liver — cross and can help with issues involving all three. DO NOT USE DURING PREGNANCY.

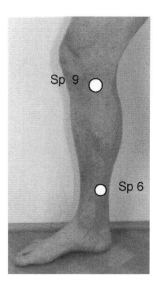

- You can hold these two points together while lying on your back; cross one leg over and place fingers onto points. Hold for one minute while taking deep, slow breaths, and then change sides.

- **CV 6 "Ocean of Ki,"** located about two finger-widths below your navel, is also good for constipation, gas, and chronic diarrhea. Place all your fingertips into this area and take slow breaths as you go deep into your lower abdomen. USE CAUTION here if you have a serious health issue or have had recent abdominal surgery.

- **K 2 "Blazing Valley,"** on the middle of the arch halfway between the outer tip of the big toe and the back of the heel, is especially good for swollen feet.

- **K 6 "Illuminated Sea,"** good with swollen ankle,s is one thumb-width below the inside of the anklebone.

- You can hold these points together also. Lying on your back with your left leg over the right, use your left finger to press K 6 on your left foot and your right thumb to press K 2 on your arch. Breathe and hold for one minute before changing sides.

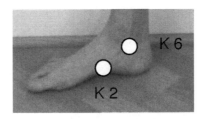

There are nutritional ways we can help to rid the body of excess water. Eating aduki beans stimulates the kidneys to promote urination. Aromatic foods and herbs—especially with pungent flavor like garlic, radish, ginger, peppermint, or with bitter flavor like asparagus, celery, coffee, dandelion greens, vinegar, tea, and hops—increase perspiration. Sweet flavor, like apples, barley, beef, chicken, corn, honey, milk, yam, and tofu, promotes urination. Cinnamon increases perspiration and promotes urine production.

If you want a healthy Spleen, you have to eat good food. The spleen is responsible for sending nutrients from the stomach to all the organs and for expelling excess body fluid. If the Spleen isn't working well, water is retained in the body. Spleen deficiency can be caused by lack of movement, overwork, overthinking, or worry.

Chapter 31
Worry

I am someone who strives to live in the present, which is one of the reasons I have trouble with the concept of worry. Lots of my friends and family are worriers though. Worry focuses on the past or the future but not on the present. A long time ago, I heard an adage by Tennessee Ernie Ford that went something like this. "Worry is like being in a rocking chair. It keeps you moving, but you don't get anywhere." Those words have kept me alert to losing myself to obsessive thinking.

In Traditional Chinese Medicine, over-caring leads to worry, which is considered an imbalance in Earth energy affecting Spleen and Stomach. Using any of the exercises to balance Spleen and Stomach will help with worry. I'm sure you've heard of being "sick with worry." A healthy concern for others can degenerate into an obsessive anxiety which causes stomach energies to stagnate, creating laziness, inertia, edema, inefficient digestion, ulcers, and a "heavy spirit."

Here are some points to help stabilize the mind and clear obsessive thoughts:

- Hold **GV 16 "Wind Mansion"** lightly for one to three minutes. It's found at the base of the skull in the center hollow.

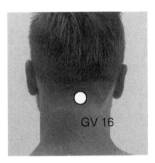

- **St 36 "Three Mile Point"** is good for helping with self-doubt and worry. Use your fists to briskly rub these points along the outside of your shin below your knee for a minute.

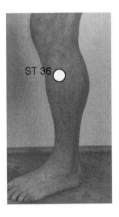

- **Lu 1 "Letting Go"** helps with letting go of worrisome thoughts while you breathe deeply for two minutes. Cross your hands on your upper chest and place your middle fingers in the soft area near your shoulders, releasing your worry with the sound "aah."

- Place your palms two finger-widths below your navel, resting on **CV 6 "Ocean of Ki."** Spend ten minutes here breathing deeply with eyes closed, letting yourself completely relax.

Another wonderful technique I learned to help with worry is to place your fingers on your forehead and place your thumbs at the center of your cheek while thinking about what you are obsessing over. Hold the thought and your head until you feel pulsing in your fingertips or have trouble holding onto the worry.

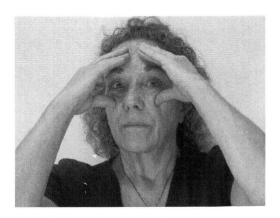

Appendix

Afterthoughts

When I mention to people that I'm working on a self-help book for dealing with the effects of Lyme disease, almost every person has told me they know of someone or several someones infected with Lyme disease. Many people have stories about themselves or the plight of another and tell me they no longer go into the woods, go hiking, or garden because they are afraid of being bitten. I can't imagine living without being in nature, but I understand completely. I know I spend less time working in my garden. I'm also not as eager to prune trees and shrubs as I used to be, especially when I have to get into the brush to do it. And I'm much more vigilant about checking for ticks.

My compassion for people challenged by Lyme disease and/or the various co-infections is great. I have faced, and continue to face, some of the effects of my Lyme experience. While researching the book, I learned that I still carry some of the residuals, most of them cognitive. When I was sick I lost the ability to walk or stand, and my muscles lost the memory and strength to do certain things. One was going up our spiral stairway. For months I went up stairs backwards on my hands. It took retraining my mind to remember how to go up our stairs using my legs. Our stairway is no longer a problem for me, but every now and again I notice I still face a moment before going up a long flight of stairs when I have to remind myself that I *do know* how to go up stairs. The same thing happens in Yoga when I move from lunge to standing in the Salutation to the Sun pose. My left leg needs a mental reminder, if not a helping hand.

Recently, my back ached terribly and then my right leg lost strength. I could hardly pick it up off the ground and knew it was my psoas muscle, the same one affected by Lyme. I had to fight the panic that rushed through me thinking it was a recurrence or a new infection. It felt a bit like PTSD with a flashback to what was. I used a few calming techniques to bring me back to the now and called Carrie who does hot stone massage to schedule a session. Gratefully, she was able to release the pain and bring back the muscle strength. I breathed a sigh of relief.

And so my journey with Lyme continues, which is why I have felt driven to offer these self-help tools to empower you, the reader, to better cope with the physical and emotional challenges from Lyme disease. I hope you find it a helpful resource for your well-being and peace of mind.

With gratitude and blessings,
Helene

References

Beinfield, Harriet, L.Ac. and Korngold, Efrem, L.Ac., O.M.D., *Between Heaven and Earth, A Guide to Chinese Medicine,* New York: Ballantine Books, Random House Publishing Group, 1991.

Cohen, Kenneth S., *The Way of Qigong: The Art and Science of Chinese Energy Healing,* New York: Ballantine Books, Random House Publishing Group, 1997.

Eden, Donna, with Feinstein, David, Ph.D., *Energy Medicine,* England: Penguin Books Ltd., 1998, 2008.

Eden, Donna, with Feinstein, David, Ph.D., *Energy Medicine for Women,* England: Penguin Books Ltd., 2008.

Elias, Jason, L.Ac., and Ketcham, Katherine, *Chinese Medicine for Maximum Immunity,* New York: Three Rivers Press, 1998.

Feinstein, David, Ph.D., Eden, Donna , and Craig, Gary, *The Promise of Energy Psychology,* New York: Tarcher/Penguin, 2005.

Gach, Michael Reed, Ph.D., and Henning, Beth Ann, Dipl., A.B.T., *Acupressure for Emotional Healing,* New York: Bantam Dell, 2004.

Gach, Michael Reed, Ph.D., *Acupressure's Potent Points,* New York: Bantam Books, 1990.

Giacomini, Teresa, *Glossary, Five Years of Workshop Notes: Learning Donna Eden's Energy Medicine,* Oregon: www.VisionaryArtByTeresa.com.

Haas, Elson M., MD, *Staying Healthy with the Seasons,* California: Celestial Arts, 1981.

Kaneko, DoAnn T., L.A.c., Ph.D., O.M.D., *Shiatsu Amna Therapy Doann's Short and Long Forms,* Shiatsu Massage School of California, Santa Monica, California, 2004.

Kaptchuk, Tej J., *The Web That Has No Weaver, Understanding Chinese Medicine,* Chicago, Illinois:, Congdon & Weed, Inc., 1983.

Kushi, Michio, *The Do-In Way,* New York: Square One Publishers, 2007.

Muramoto, Naboru, *Healing Ourselves,* New York: Swan House Publishing Company, 1973.

Manaka, Yoshio, MD, and Urquhart, Ian A., Ph.D., *The Layman's Guide to Acupuncture,* New York: Weatherhill, 1975.

Mann, Felix, M.B., *Acupuncture - The Ancient Chinese Art of Healing and How it Works Scientifically,* New York: Vintage, 1973.

Muramoto, Naboru, *Healing Ourselves,* New York: Swan House Publishing Company, 1973.

Reichstein, Gail, *Wood Becomes Water - Chinese Medicine in Everyday Life,* New York: Kodansha America, Inc., 1998.

Serizawa, Katsusuke, MD, *Tsubo Vital Points for Oriental Therapy,* Tokyo, Japan:Japan Publications, Inc., 1976.

Teeguarden, Iona Marsaa, *Acupressure Way of Health: jin shin do,* Tokyo, Japan: Japan Publications, Inc., 1978.

Thie, John D.C., and Thie, Matthew, M.Ed, *Touch for Health: The Complete Edition,* California: DeVorss & Company, 2005, www.devorss.com.

Veith, Ilza, *The Yellow Emperor's Classic of Internal Medicine,* California: University of California Press, 1949.

Walker, Lauren, *Energy Medicine Yoga,* Sounds True, 2014.

Classes from:

Vicki Matthews

Donna Eden

Mary Sise

Websites:

http://www.acupuncture.com/

www.acupunctureproducts.com

https://bigtreehealing.com

www.centerfortraditionalmedicine.org

http://www.harmonygate.com

www.innersource.net

www.spavietnam.com

http://www.TCMStudent.com The World of Acupuncture and
    Oriental Medicine

www.TheTappingSolution.com

http://www.yinyanghouse.com

About the author

Helene Brecker has been studying various modalities of healing since the mid-1970s. That's when she began her journey with Shiatsu and theories of Japanese medicine. She added Touch for Health and reflexology to her studies and practice. After a hiatus for graduate school and years as a Clinical Social Worker, she discovered and trained in Thought Field Therapy, an Energy Psychology technique. This led her to begin years of study with Donna Eden and Vicki Matthews, ND, and she attained certification in Eden Energy Medicine in 2007. Helene has taught classes in Shiatsu, yoga, and Energy Medicine and incorporates her various modalities into her practice. For more information, check her website: helenebrecker.abmp.com.

Helene's goal is to "empower people with the skills and awareness that the power of healing is in their hands."

29681845R00099

Made in the USA
Middletown, DE
27 February 2016